akiya
空き家

Simply put, akiya means "empty house."

To tackle the renovation of an old and fading property requires bravery as well as vision.

To do that in a foreign country - where the language is an obstacle and regulations, paperwork and local approaches to such a project are completely alien to anything you have experienced before—requires an entirely different level of fortitude.

Anton Wörmann has created a warm, stylish and comfortable home out of a tumbledown shack; a remarkable achievement. He freely admits there were good days and bad days on the building site, but this book will help anyone else who is considering buying a Japanese "akiya" and giving it a new lease of life.

It's almost as if he has done all the heavy lifting for us.

—Julian Ryall, The Daily Telegraph

FREE HOUSES IN JAPAN

THE TRUE STORY OF HOW I MAKE MONEY
DIY RENOVATING ABANDONED HOMES

Anton Wörmann

illustrated by Megan Douglas

🏠 Anton in Japan Media

ISBN 979-8-9890955-0-6 (Paperback Edition)
ISBN 979-8-9890955-1-3 (eBook Edition)

First Paperback Edition: November 2023

Book Design by Hafiz Khairul
Illustrated by Megan Douglas
Copyediting by Patrick Merritt & Angela Grace
Publishing Consulting & Services by Bookener:
www.bookener.com

To Daisuke Maeda, my first modeling manager:
thank you for bringing me to Japan. Bruce, your knowledge
about Tokyo real estate was a game-changer. Kazuki-san, I'm
grateful for your teachings on Japanese carpentry. Isozaki-san,
your introduction to the akiya investment community was a
turning point.

And to Lia, your constant support during my crazy
renovation adventures means the world.

Contents

Part 3: RENOVATING

Part 4: MONETIZING

Part 5: RESOURCES

FREE HOUSES IN JAPAN

THE TRUE STORY OF HOW I MAKE MONEY DIY RENOVATING ABANDONED HOMES

ANTON'S JOURNEY

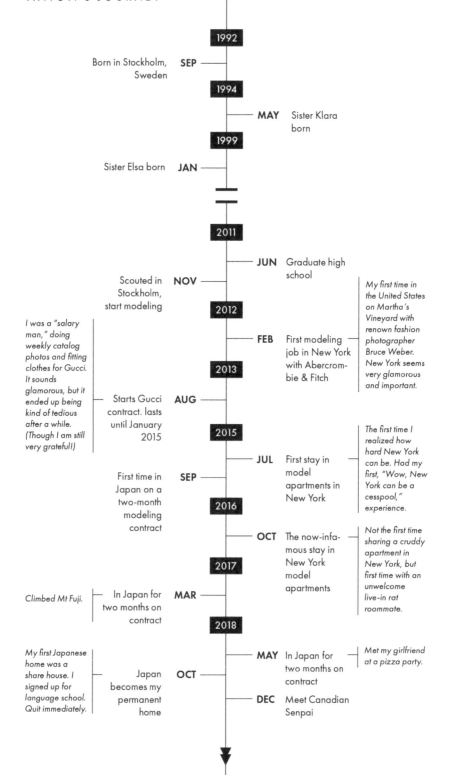

1992

SEP — Born in Stockholm, Sweden

1994

MAY — Sister Klara born

1999

JAN — Sister Elsa born

2011

JUN — Graduate high school

NOV — Scouted in Stockholm, start modeling

2012

FEB — First modeling job in New York with Abercrombie & Fitch

My first time in the United States on Martha's Vineyard with renown fashion photographer Bruce Weber. New York seems very glamorous and important.

2013

I was a "salary man," doing weekly catalog photos and fitting clothes for Gucci. It sounds glamorous, but it ended up being kind of tedious after a while. (Though I am still very grateful!)

AUG — Starts Gucci contract. lasts until January 2015

2015

JUL — First stay in model apartments in New York

The first time I realized how hard New York can be. Had my first, "Wow, New York can be a cesspool," experience.

SEP — First time in Japan on a two-month modeling contract

2016

OCT — The now-infamous stay in New York model apartments

Not the first time sharing a cruddy apartment in New York, but first time with an unwelcome live-in rat roommate.

2017

Climbed Mt Fuji. — In Japan for two months on contract

MAR

2018

MAY — In Japan for two months on contract — *Met my girlfriend at a pizza party.*

My first Japanese home was a share house. I signed up for language school. Quit immediately. — Japan becomes my permanent home

OCT

DEC — Meet Canadian Senpai

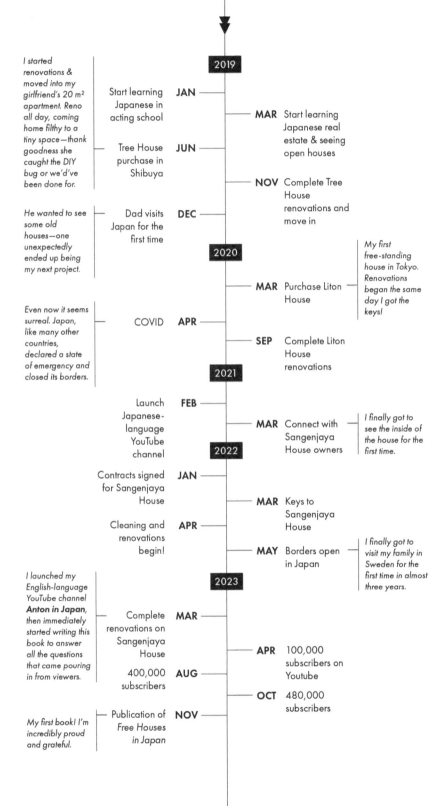

2019

JAN — Start learning Japanese in acting school

I started renovations & moved into my girlfriend's 20 m² apartment. Reno all day, coming home filthy to a tiny space—thank goodness she caught the DIY bug or we'd've been done for.

MAR Start learning Japanese real estate & seeing open houses

JUN — Tree House purchase in Shibuya

NOV Complete Tree House renovations and move in

DEC — Dad visits Japan for the first time

He wanted to see some old houses—one unexpectedly ended up being my next project.

2020

MAR Purchase Liton House

My first free-standing house in Tokyo. Renovations began the same day I got the keys!

APR — COVID

Even now it seems surreal. Japan, like many other countries, declared a state of emergency and closed its borders.

SEP Complete Liton House renovations

2021

FEB — Launch Japanese-language YouTube channel

MAR Connect with Sangenjaya House owners

I finally got to see the inside of the house for the first time.

2022

JAN — Contracts signed for Sangenjaya House

MAR Keys to Sangenjaya House

APR — Cleaning and renovations begin!

MAY Borders open in Japan

I finally got to visit my family in Sweden for the first time in almost three years.

2023

MAR — Complete renovations on Sangenjaya House

I launched my English-language YouTube channel **Anton in Japan**, then immediately started writing this book to answer all the questions that came pouring in from viewers.

APR 100,000 subscribers on Youtube

AUG — 400,000 subscribers

OCT 480,000 subscribers

NOV — Publication of Free Houses in Japan

My first book! I'm incredibly proud and grateful.

Foreword

Hi! My name is Anton. I live in Japan, but I am originally from Stockholm, Sweden. My adventure in Japan started back in 2015 when I came here for my work as a fashion model. I've lived and worked in cities all over the US and Europe—New York, Paris, London, Milan—and when I came here for the first time, I had no idea that Japan would capture my heart and become my home.

If I could time-travel a decade into the past and tell myself that in ten years I'd be living in Tokyo, speaking fluent Japanese, making YouTube videos, and buying and renovating old houses, I wouldn't have believed it.

Well, maybe I'd have believed the renovating part. Growing up in Älvsjö, a southern suburb of Stockholm, my family lived in a fixer-upper built in 1909. To save money my Dad did the renovations himself and he worked on the house from when I was little until I was a teenager. My two younger sisters and I would take the leftover wood and build tiny little houses in the garden. Something an American kid would probably call a "fort." Renovating is in my blood.

But Japan?

Although, looking back on it now, there was much more Japanese influence on my childhood in Sweden than I was aware of at the time. Nintendo, Toyota, Honda, Toshiba, Sony, Nikon, Canon—I had no idea these were all Japanese imports we were using every day. In middle school there were also these kids with pink hair and weird t-shirts that were obsessed with all things Japanese. I didn't get it then, but now I know they were on to something. We all loved Dragon Ball Z and Pokemon. I'm not sure what was more exciting—the stories or the fact that the pages of the book turned from right to left instead of the typical left to right we were used to. So exotic.

The thing I remember most is my Mom's love of sushi. Like I said, I grew up with two younger sisters and we always ate at home. We went grocery shopping about once a week and my parents cooked meals at home every night. Eating out in a restaurant was incredibly rare—a special treat. Every so often, just a few times a year, when my Dad was away from home, my Mom would treat us to sushi from Fruängen, the local Japanese takeout restaurant. We'd get some California rolls and maybe an eight-piece sushi plate and eat it at home with the chopsticks my Mom kept in the silverware drawer. It was so expensive and I'm not sure that any of us kids really understood why Mom loved it so much, but it felt special to be sharing her favorite food and seeing how happy it made her.

Later, when I started modeling, I met so many people who were into Japanese fashion, craftsmanship, and materials. I heard from models who had worked in Japan that the pay was good, the food was

great, and the way they treated
the models was exceptional.
I started to think I was really
missing out on something.
So, when I got that invitation
to come to Japan for the first
time, back in 2015, I immediately said yes.

I had always assumed
that the Big Apple—New
York City—would be my
ultimate destination. But after my first trip to Japan, I
couldn't get Japan out
of my mind. I came back
twice more for work, and
each time when my contract was up and it was time to go, I
would have this overwhelming feeling that I didn't want to leave.
When I worked in other countries I would compare them to Japan,
wishing I was back here. Eventually, at the end of 2018, I was able to
move here permanently. I've never looked back.

Within a year after moving here I bought the Tree House. My
first property! I renovated it in true DIY style. When I finished that
one, I found another, Liton House, which I now live in. Then a
third, Sangenjaya House, the house renovation that's featured on
my YouTube channel playlist *Tokyo Renovation Diaries*.

Originally, I made videos about the renovation in Japanese so
I could practice my language skills. I started publishing them on
YouTube in 2021 on a Japanese-language channel. I never expected

there would be interest in European/American-style DIY renovations with a Japanese-speaking audience. Given how small the DIY culture is here (more on that later) it was a surprise. There was so much interest that in 2023 I decided to launch an English-language channel on YouTube, *Anton in Japan*.

My first video went viral with over 30 million views, and within four months the subscriber list topped 400,000. Questions and comments poured in on every video. I had no idea that there would be so much interest in this unusual thing I was doing.

I am so incredibly thankful to everyone for being so supportive and asking so many questions. You are the reason I decided to share my knowledge and expertise regarding buying and renovating old houses in Japan. I'm having fun and making a living while doing it. This book, my first book, is a culmination of the tens of thousands of comments and interactions I've had with you across my YouTube channels. Your engagement and curiosity have shaped this work, and I couldn't be more grateful.

Thank you for being a part of this incredible journey.
—Anton (in Japan)

How This Story Began

My first flight from Stockholm to Tokyo was over sixteen hours including a layover in Beijing. Having landed in Japan for the first time ever, I was exhausted, hungry, and nervous, but also excited. I had been hired to work in Japan for two months as a fashion model. I had no idea what to expect. But I was definitely not expecting that this short modeling contract would lead to me buying and renovating abandoned homes in Japan a few years down the road. On that day, back in September of 2015, all I knew was that I was about to meet my Japanese modeling agent and get my measurements taken.

Modeling contracts in Japan are different from anywhere in Europe or America. The agency guarantees you a minimum amount of pay while you are there to work. This is very unusual.

In return you guarantee that you will keep your hair the same, your skin in condition, do the jobs you're booked for, follow the rules, be well behaved, and, most importantly, maintain your measurements. They take your measurements when you arrive and every week you're there to make sure they haven't changed.

It sounds a little oppressive, but the agency has taken the risk of bringing you to Japan and guaranteeing your $10,000 paycheck for two months' work. They need to know that if they can't book you for work that they will be able to keep that money. So, I knew they were going to measure me when I arrived. I was so afraid they'd say my measurements had changed and send me back home that I hadn't eaten the entire flight.

I now know that they almost never have to send a model home or break their contract. The models are chosen carefully by the agency and brought to Japan because they believe in them and the work they do. In my case, I had been modeling for four years in the US and Europe, including two years as the "Gucci Boy," the exclusive model for Gucci. When Daisuke Maeda scouted me in Europe in 2015, he knew he could book me practically on name recognition alone; there were clients that would want me to work for them just because I'd worked for Gucci, even without seeing my face.

But on that day back in 2015, when the agency driver, Yuki-san, came to pick me up at the terminal after traveling for over twenty hours, I was nervous. He said we had to take fresh snaps right there in the airport for the booking agents and all I could think was, "I must look a wreck." We drove to the agency to say hello to Maeda-san and the other agents and have all of my measurements taken. I was so new and spoke so little Japanese I didn't dare talk to any of the other agents at the time.

After my measurements were taken they walked me over to the model apartments where I'd be staying for my two-month contract. Model apartments need a bit of explanation. These are apartments that the modeling agency provides to the models they employ. The rent is deducted from your pay—very convenient, very easy, and when the contract is over the model can leave for the next city without having to worry about quitting any sort of rental contract. Model apartments are **also** a great way for the agency to keep track of their models. In Japan, this is especially important with foreign models who might not understand Japan, Japanese manners, or Japanese culture at all. Model apartments give the modeling agency an easy way to keep track of, and keep an eye on, their models.

Most models are very professional, but there's always one who seems to always be in trouble. I've seen it a hundred times. A foreign model misinterpreting a curious gaze from a local as a challenge to a brawl? Seen that. Forgetting basic Japanese etiquette and causing a neighborhood fight? Seen that too. Getting belligerent because the 24-hour convenience store is open but the restroom inside is locked? Yep. That one ended up with the police being called and the agency having to send someone to smooth things over and explain to the model (who had had too many sakes) that the restrooms are locked at 11pm every night, even in the 24-hour stores.

The agency provides apartments, transportation, and managers to chaperone their charges from place to place, keeping the models close at hand and intervening if there's a problem.

That first day, my manager walked me over to the building where my model apartment was, just a block away from the agency in Roppongi. On the way he filled me in on everything I needed to know, then gave me the keys and showed me the front door to the building.

I was very hungry, so before I went up to my apartment, I went into the Family Mart located on the ground floor of the building.

I still remember the smells and impressions walking into a Japanese convenience store for the first time in my life: the sliding doors opening and the Family Mart jingle going on simultaneously "Di di di di di di, di di di di di di." By the cash register there was oden (おでん), a Japanese stew in a dashi broth, that made the whole store smell warm and fishy. Let's just say I'm not a big fan of oden. I bought myself a two-liter bottle of water and something I thought was chicken, along with some salted cashew nuts, and took the elevator up to apartment 702.

I was pleasantly surprised at the charming, little space. The building was built in the 1980s, fairly new by American standards, old by Japanese standards. The room was very small—the door frame to enter the room was only about 175 cm (5' 9") high—I had to crouch when entering. The kitchen corner had a cooking plate and a stainless steel sink. The shower and toilet was a traditional Japanese unit bathroom in yellow-ish plastic.* There was a single bed, a small chair, a plastic desk, a TV, a tiny fridge, some small baskets for trash, and a big closet. The windows were facing the Mercedes Benz showroom, and the Benz logo lit up the Tokyo evening. It was one of the best model apartments I've ever stayed in. Tiny, clean, no rats, centrally located, no sharing with some random dude. It was perfect. So much better than model apartments in New York or Milan.

I mentioned New York. Did I also mention rats?

---

* Japanese unit bathrooms are similar to prefab shower unit kits in the United States, except instead of just the shower, it includes the entire bathroom; sink, tub, and toilet.

When people hear you're a model living in New York, they assume you're living in some swanky penthouse with panoramic views of the city. Nope. Most of the model apartments are bottom-of-the-barrel, shoddy places you'd never imagine stepping foot in, let alone calling home. I stayed in one that was a stone's throw from the Empire State Building with moldy walls, and—wait for it—rats. Inside. I know, it's New York. You'd think we'd be used to seeing rats everywhere. But having one in your living space? That's a whole different ball game.

There were four of us crammed into this tiny apartment—Will, Dylan, Jegor, and myself. Four guys sharing two tiny bedrooms and a "living room" that was more like a closet. Plus the rat, who apparently considered himself our fifth roommate. This thing would come out at night, and he was not shy, either. He'd dig through the trash bags and eat whatever he found. We tried putting our food on high shelves. Fail. We tried putting it in garbage bags. Fail. Finally, we put everything edible in the fridge to keep it safe—even the cereal.

The agency didn't seem to care—they just told us to buy a trap. Not helpful. We tried everything to get him out. Every night just as we'd be falling asleep: rustle, rustle, rustle. Then we'd all get up and try to chase him out but he'd scuttle down some hidey-hole and it was back to bed. Then, just as we were falling asleep again: rustle, rustle, rustle. One night, in sheer desperation, we got a broom and tried to herd him out the front door. Can you imagine it? Four grown men chasing a rat around a tiny, crappy New York apartment with a broom in the dead of night. (Fail.)

Eventually we gave up and learned to ignore the noise, roll over, and go back to sleep. We lived like that for a month until our contracts were up at the December holidays. Two of us went back home, and two of us were moved to a different apartment for new modeling contracts.

Yes, you heard that right. The four of us moved out and the rat stayed.

When I got to Tokyo, I was ready for the same ordeal, but to my astonishment and great relief, Tokyo was different. My model apartment was clean, cozy, and best of all, vermin-free. I looked around the cute space, tired and hungry but happy and at home in my snug little spot. I sat down by the desk and opened what I thought was chicken and was met with the worst smell you can imagine. To this day I don't know exactly how to describe it. Imagine rotten cabbage mixed with . . . fish? In high school I worked in a supermarket and sometimes customers would complain about getting meat that had gone bad. The smell of these returned packages of bad meat might be the closest smell I can think of. I suspect that what I had thought was chicken was actually some kind of fermented eel, which is still not my favorite, but on that night back in 2015, there was no way I was going to eat it. I didn't know what to do with it. I couldn't just put it in the trash in my room—I would have been smelling that smell for the next two months. Now I know I could have gone down and thrown it in the trash at the Family Mart, but I didn't know that then. I opened the small window and hid the "chicken" on the sill. Window closed, smell contained. Success! A week later it had magically disappeared. To this day I don't know what happened to it.

In the end, my first meal in Japan was a few cashew nuts before passing out from exhaustion. Fortunately for me I had a much better experience with food a few days later.

When working as a model, the agency will drive groups of models to and from auditions for bookings, called "castings." Everyone calls this the "casting car," and we all spend a lot of time together in it. That particular trip I'd spent a lot of time in the casting car with my new friend Gavin. Gavin is from Florida and had come to Japan ten years prior to study Japanese and attend a Japanese university. He got scouted in the street in Shibuya Crossing (渋谷スクランブル 交差点). Now he's a comedian, but back then he was a model and after a particularly long day in the casting car he suggested we go to a favorite spot of his, a restaurant called Secchan (せっちゃん).

We hopped onto a subway—my first ever in Japan, mind you, a nerve-wracking experience in itself. Fifteen minutes later, we arrived at what felt like a remote, countryside diner, which was in fact, smack in the middle of the city, in Shimokitazawa (下北沢).

When we walked in I immediately recognized the signature scent of an izakaya (居酒屋), a pub, through a haze of smoke from the flat iron frying griddles, teppan (鉄板), on every table. We would order, the chef would prepare the food, and then he'd hand it over for us to cook ourselves, right at our table. I had okonomiyaki (お 好み焼き) for the first time that night—a savory Japanese pancake made of cabbage and eggs, smothered in a uniquely sweet sauce that I thought tasted something like a mix of Worcestershire sauce and mayonnaise. We fried up smoked cheese and many other things. It was an unforgettable meal. To this day I still take friends to Secchan when they come to visit me in Japan, and I always take some of the sauce back to Sweden so I can cook okonomiyaki for my mom.

That night, amidst the sizzle, the laughter, the clinking glasses and all the stories that Gavin shared with me—each one unfolding another layer of this mesmerizing country—I didn't just fall for okonomiyaki; I fell deeply in love with Japan.

And then there was Norman.

Norman, my Japanese friend that I got to know in Finland. Yes, Finland. Our first meeting was actually in Sweden, a two-minute introduction to each other at the modeling agency. The next day I headed to Finland for the very first time to go to a music festival with some friends. I missed my first flight, so I had to go straight from the airport to the festival with just my backpack to meet up with everyone. One of my friends and I got in line for the toilet, and he asked to borrow my phone to call his girlfriend. "Sure," I said, handing it over. And then he vanished. Like smoke. There I was, alone in a sea of 50,000 festival-goers—in a country I'd never been to—with no friends and no phone. I tried asking strangers to dial my number, hoping I'd hear the ringtone and find my friend again, but no luck.

Just as I was about to give up, this Japanese guy tapped me on the shoulder and said, "Weren't you in Sweden yesterday?" It was Norman. We hung out the rest of the evening, and I finally found my friends at the end of the night.

A year later, I moved to Japan and Norman and I had some crazy adventures. Every outing with him was a surprise. He'd say we were going to the arcade, but then we'd be in the countryside, or jamming in Yoyogi Park. Or we'd join in on the Cinco de Mayo festival put on in Tokyo to celebrate Latin American culture. Except, in Japanese, "cinco" sounds exactly like a slang term for a certain male body part, so things would get a little out of hand. Or we'd take the subway up to Shinjuku (新宿区), stumble into some karaoke (カラオケ) place with cosplay costumes at the entrance, and the night would end with Mario belting out ballads, Yoshi doing a rap, and a cow having a duet with a Japanese schoolgirl.

Japan was like stepping into a world where every day was an unexpected adventure. Walk down any street and it could transform into the most surreal night of your life. Like the times a local would pull me and my friends into some bar we'd never seen before. We'd laugh, drink, and dance, feeling like we were in the best place on earth. But after that night we'd never be able to find that bar again.

Twice more over the next three years I came back to Japan for two-month modeling contracts, and I always stayed in the model apartments in Roppongi. I had already fallen in love with the food and during these additional trips I fell in love with the convenience and the culture. In Japan, you can walk out of your door and everything you could possibly want is available 24/7 just a short walk away. Japan is like New York, but safe.

Then there's the culture. The Japanese are a study in respect and reverence. Honesty is a way of life. Forget your wallet on a bench? It's likely to be returned with everything intact. Everyone follows the rules, and queues up when required. It's orderly in a way that's hard to understand until you experience it. The intricacies of social norms and etiquette can be baffling. Like the custom of pouring drinks for people of a higher social status than you at the table, and making sure their glass is always full. Even after five years, I've learned so much and yet still so much is a mystery, but that is part of what makes it so intriguing.

If you get it wrong and pour the wrong person's drink, you will definitely get a funny look. Fortunately foreigners are given the "gai-jin (外人) card"—an understanding that you might not get things right because you are a foreigner. As long as you show respect and genuinely try, the Japanese are more than forgiving.

On my third trip, in 2018, I met my girlfriend. In a pizza restaurant in Roppongi.

A friend of mine was about to leave Japan so they had a pizza party and there were about twenty people, a mix of foreigners and Japanese. I wanted to practice the language so I started talking to this pretty girl in my bad Japanese. I thought she was fluent. Turns out she is Korean and her Japanese was bad, too. But neither of us knew that then. The next week I took her to Secchan—the same restaurant that Gavin had taken me to years before—and we've been together ever since.

It's hard to explain how captivated by this country I was after only three trips. I just knew that every time I was about to leave Japan, I wasn't ready to leave. Each time I had to pack my bags, there was a voice inside saying, "Please, let me stay just a little bit longer."

I decided it was time to make Japan my permanent home.

Once I decided to live here full-time, I knew I wanted to find my own place, not stay in the model apartments. I wasn't a kid anymore at 26! I asked my manager, Maeda-san, for suggestions on where to live. He suggested a share house, which has become increasingly popular in Japan. You typically have your own room but share the kitchen and common areas. Intrigued by the idea, I decided to look into it and found a charming share house close to Harajuku (原宿).

The owner of the share house, Shingo-san, proved to be a wealth of knowledge about real estate in Japan. It was also around this time that I met my mentor, Canadian Senpai (先輩). I'll tell you all about him later. The insights I gained from Shingo-san, Canadian Senpai, and others have been invaluable in navigating the real estate landscape in Japan.

As I settled into life in Tokyo, juggling my modeling gigs a few days a week and immersing myself in daily Japanese language learning, my curiosity for the world of Japanese houses grew immensely. With each passing day, I found myself falling more and more in love with the idea of establishing deeper roots in this captivating country. It was time to find a place of my own—no roommates.

When I looked into getting my own place, I was shocked at how much money I would need to rent a small apartment. I have lived all over the world—New York, Australia, London, Milan and more. I have never seen a more complex rental market, with more outrageous fees and costs, than the one in Tokyo. In some cases you have to pay up to half a year's rent in fees, up front. Money that in most cases you will never get back. Gratitude money, key money, renewal fees . . . oh, and being charged thousands of dollars for putting a small pin-hole in the wallpaper from hanging a photo of loved ones (more on that later).

Turns out it is often easier and cheaper to buy a place in Japan than it is to rent one. And I knew that if I owned my home in Japan, I could also use the talents I'd practiced since I was a kid in Sweden—renovating and reviving.

I took a look at my finances and decided to find a place to buy instead.

I bought the Tree House a few months later.

That's how this story began.

Part 1
PREPARING

🔑 1

Learning the Market

There are over 8.5 million abandoned homes in Japan,
and the average age of a home when it is torn down is
only 32.1 years.

When I first laid eyes on my "Tree House" apartment near Shibuya, I knew it was the one. The building's perfect location on the top floor with big, bright windows in three directions created a fantastic atmosphere. Plus, the small ladder leading up to the loft added a unique charm. There were a couple of downsides, however. No elevator, and the building, by Japanese standards, was quite old.

The apartment was 39 m² (420 ft²) in size and the price was around ¥14 million ($96,552).* I couldn't believe how cheap it

---

* For consistency, we have set an exchange rate of ¥145 per $1 throughout the book, and all dollar amounts are United States dollars. As currency exchange rates vary daily, the current exchange rate at the time you are reading this book is likely different.

was. In Stockholm, Sweden, I couldn't even buy a parking lot for that money, and here I was, in the heart of Tokyo, just a quick bike ride away from the famous Shibuya Crossing (渋谷スクランブル交差点).

Japanese real estate pamphlets often lack interior pictures, leaving you in suspense until you visit the property in person. The moment I stepped inside, I could tell that the place needed some serious renovation. The small kitchen at the entrance smelled bad, and it seemed like no maintenance had been done in ages. But I was undeterred; the limiting factors could be fixed with an easy renovation.

When I showed pictures and videos of the apartment to my foreign friends from America and Europe, they couldn't believe what a great deal it was. "ONLY 100K?! YOU HAVE TO GET IT! GET IT NOW!"

But when I showed the same to my Japanese friends, they looked at me with concern and caution. "It's pretty old, huh? Are you sure about this? Will they clean the place before you get the keys?" they asked, more risk-averse than my foreign friends.

On the second visit, I brought my Korean girlfriend along to share in my excitement.

When we arrived outside the building, I could already tell this wasn't going to go well. Her face looked like she had just sucked on a lemon and smelled something bad at the same time. At the entrance to the apartment she took one look inside and asked the broker why it was so dirty.

"Are they going to clean the place before we get the keys?" she asked.

I thought she was being incredibly rude. "We can fix it ourselves," I said, adding, "your energy is really bad."

She shot back, "It's dirty, it's old and I **don't** want to be associated **with this**."

She refused to come in, her legs and arms compressed together to keep the dirty apartment from touching her. It was like I had taken her to the slimiest, sleaziest, scuzziest trailer park you could imagine and said, "Look, babe, this is our new home, isn't it great?" and she responded, "Are you insane? I will never, **ever** bring any friends here. I will **never** bring my family here. No one will ever, ever, **EVER** know that I live here."

I told her to go wait outside while I looked at the apartment again. This place was gold covered in trash. How can she not see this?

Meanwhile (I now know) she was thinking, "This is going to **destroy** my reputation, how can he not see this?"

What's funny is, since then we've had bigger fights over smaller things. She didn't like it, but at some level she knew that I had a vision, that this was my choice, and this was something I **had** to do. As big of a life-changing decision as this was—buying an apartment after only living in the country for a few months—she supported me in doing it. She didn't help at first, and she definitely didn't understand it, but she didn't try to change my mind.

I made the purchase and we moved in together to her 20 m² (215 ft²) apartment in order to save money. She helped a little with the initial clean up, but then the very dirty demo work began and I was on my own. On the days I wasn't modeling I would return to our shared and very small apartment completely filthy. Can you imagine how excited she was?

But when we started to paint and decorate, she started to get involved. When she saw the apartment coming together so beautifully, she was blown away. She hadn't realized that you could do these things—that they were even possible. Now she's as excited as I am to look at old, dirty houses. We're a team. She sees it, understands it, and has the vision. Now when I take her to a dirty, abandoned old house, she's like: ***"Let's DO IT!"***

Now that I've spent more time in Japan, I also understand better why she had that less-than-positive reaction to the Tree House apartment. The Japanese have very different feelings and beliefs about older homes than people in the United States and Europe.

Tokyo has limited space and the way Japanese people live and spend their lives is very different from anywhere else. Japanese architecture is beautiful and renowned all over the world, and I love looking at these old, beautiful Japanese kominkas (古民家) and temples. Simply a work of art. But what do Japanese people prioritize in their homes?

I have seen and been to a vast amount of Japanese houses, apartments, and condos—what the Japanese call manshons (マンション)—mostly in and around Tokyo: small windows, nearby buildings blocking the sunlight, big fluorescent panel lights in the ceiling, walls covered in the same trending white wallpaper, vinyl flooring, unit bathroom, unit kitchen. Everything made to look as fresh and new as possible. Get a gouge in the floor? Have the entire floor redone in a day. Need a new kitchen? Out with the old unit kitchen and in with the latest one. Takes the contractor a day or two. The apartment is easy to maintain and it looks nice, but most importantly to a Japanese buyer or tenant: it looks ***New***.

Plus, this building will probably be torn down in 25–30 years, so why bother making it personal?

OVERVIEW OF THE SITUATION IN JAPAN

In Japan, the perspective on home value is quite different from many other countries. While older homes often hold historical and aesthetic value in other places, in Japan, newly-built homes are highly preferred. This perspective stems from the belief that the land itself holds greater value than the aging structure, particularly in light of new regulations addressing earthquake safety. The government has even set a fixed-term depreciation period of twenty-two years, so homes in Japan are literally worth nothing after twenty-two years.[*]

The trend of demolishing and rebuilding homes is also deeply rooted in Japan's history, influenced by post-World War II construction techniques and updated building codes to withstand earthquakes and natural disasters. People expect the house to lose value quickly, resulting in little motivation to maintain them for potential future buyers. As a result, the country has a large number of registered architects due to the constant demand for custom-built homes.

So what contributes to this cultural norm of always rebuilding new homes? Fires, earthquakes and a housing bubble that burst.

Fires

Throughout its history, Tokyo has been no stranger to devastating fires. From the early days of Edo to the modern city of Tokyo, fires have posed a constant threat. The city's dense layout, with houses situated close to each other, has made fires particularly rampant and destructive.

---

[*] "Japanese Homes Aren't Built to Last—and That's the Point", Robb Report, May 8, 2021, https://robbreport.com/shelter/home-design/japanese-homes-are-ephemeral-facing-demolition-just-22-years-in-heres-why-1234608438/

One of the most significant fires in Tokyo's history was the Great Fire of Meireki in 1657, which engulfed the city and resulted in the loss of over 100,000 lives. The Great Kantō Earthquake in 1923, which triggered massive fires, wiped out entire neighborhoods. The fire-bombing of Tokyo during World War II destroyed 16 square miles (41 km2) of the city and left over a million people homeless. Each time, the city was rebuilt.

The memory of past fires remains a cautionary reminder for Japanese people. They have adopted a strong cultural awareness of fire safety. Even today, the rhythmic sound of striking wooden batons and the chant of hinoyoujin (火の用心), beware of house fires, echoes on summer evenings. As Tokyo has embraced modernization, fire safety became a primary concern. Many house builders and developers now prioritize fire safety as a main selling point. Advanced technologies, improved construction materials, and strict building codes have been implemented to minimize the risk of fires spreading rapidly.

Earthquakes

Japan is a country of earthquakes, and while we feel the trembling from time to time, I must admit, earthquakes are scary. I didn't experience the big earthquake in 2011, but I remember it vividly, reading the news in my mother's house in the suburbs of Stockholm. Years later, I visited Fukushima for a week-long photo shoot. Talking to people affected in MinamiSoma, Fukushima, really made me realize the seriousness of earthquakes and tsunamis. I would strongly recommend people who don't believe in the power of nature to search on Youtube for Fukushima 2011. The videos of the tsunami sweeping in and the clips from the shaking airport will always be in my mind. My heartfelt thoughts continue to be with all the people who went missing and lost their lives in this tragedy.

There's a 70% chance of a strong earthquake hitting Tokyo directly in the next thirty years. Researchers, led by Professor Akira Fuse from Nippon Medical School and data analysis company BrainPad, studied what could happen if people don't get medical help after such a quake. Using past data and government estimates, they found that in a severe situation, around 21,500 people could be badly hurt if an earthquake happens north of Tokyo Bay. Among these, about 6,638 people, or around 31%, might not be able to get the care they need and could die. Most of these unfortunate cases would likely be in areas with many wooden buildings. About 90% of these potential deaths might occur in parts of Tokyo's northeastern and eastern wards.[*]

Big earthquakes and evolving building techniques are the reasons why laws within building in Japan are changing. Most old buildings, especially the ones built before 1981 are not up-to-date with the latest building requirements for earthquakes and fire protection. Earthquake retrofitting has been a necessary project on all of the homes I have renovated in Japan.

Housing Bubble

During the 1980s, Japan experienced a financial and economic boom, famously known as the "Bubble Era." The period saw unprecedented growth in real estate prices, transforming Tokyo's skyline with towering skyscrapers and luxury properties. Much like the US housing bubble in 2008 that fueled the Great Recession, Japan's

---

[*] "Tokyo risks over 6,000 'untreated deaths' in major earthquake", Nikkei Asia, March 11, 2023, https://asia.nikkei.com/Economy/Natural-disasters/Tokyo-risks-over-6-000-untreated-deaths-in-major-earthquake

Bubble Era was characterized by a rapid surge in asset prices, including real estate. Land prices, particularly in Tokyo and other major cities, skyrocketed to astronomical levels. The insatiable demand for prime properties and the willingness of financial institutions to extend loans fueled the bubble's expansion, mirroring the sentiment in the US housing market during the early 2000s.

However, the Japanese housing bubble burst in the early 1990s. Speculation and excessive lending practices reached a tipping point. Overnight, property prices plummeted, leaving many investors, corporations, and financial institutions burdened with massive debts and unsellable properties.

In the aftermath of the bursting bubble, Japan experienced its "Lost Decade," a prolonged period of economic stagnation that shares parallels with the Great Recession's impact on the US economy. Real estate prices suffered prolonged deflation, leading to a subdued market and sluggish demand. This aftermath continues to shape the way Japanese people perceive the real estate market in Tokyo. Decades after the bubble burst, the memories of the unprecedented rise and subsequent devastating crash have left a lasting impact on the nation's collective psyche.

🔑

There is one abandoned home in Japan
for every person in New York City!

For many Japanese citizens, the cautionary tale of the Bubble Era serves as a stark reminder of the risks associated with speculative

Akiya (空き家) means "empty house" and is the word that the Japanese use to refer to a vacant, abandoned house. These houses have often been empty and neglected for many years, and have a huge influence on the current state of real estate in Japan.

buying and excessive lending practices. As a result, there is a prevailing sense of conservatism and prudence when it comes to real estate investments. Japanese home buyers tend to approach the market with a focus on long-term stability and practicality, rather than chasing short-lived market euphoria.

WHY ARE THERE "FREE" HOUSES IN JAPAN?

There are an estimated 8.5 million abandoned houses (akiyas) across Japan, and around 810,000 of those are in Tokyo.* For comparison, in 2021 the population of the five boroughs of New York City was 8.4 million people. The ward I live in, Setegaya—the Brooklyn of Tokyo—has nearly 50,000 abandoned homes, the highest number of any ward in Tokyo.**

---

* "What to do with Tokyo's hundreds of thousands of abandoned homes", Real Estate Japan, February 15, 2018, https://resources.realestate.co.jp/news/what-to-do-with-tokyos-hundreds-of-thousands-of-abandoned-homes/
** "Setagaya has the largest number of akiya (empty homes) in Japan", Japan Property Central, May 12, 2020, https://japanpropertycentral.com/2020/05/

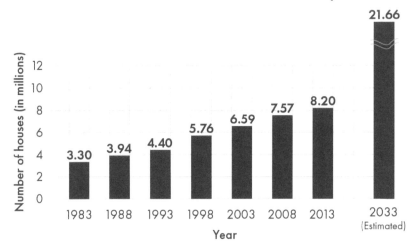

Number of Abandoned Houses in Japan

Why are there so many "free" homes in Japan? *(They are not really free, as many claim, but they are very, **very** inexpensive.)* Why can you find so many inexpensive abandoned houses in Japan? Deflation, depreciation, and a declining population are three key factors.

Deflation

Japan is the third-largest economy in the world, also measured in real estate value, and it boasts a rich history of innovation and prosperity. However, the past few decades have seen the nation grapple with prolonged economic stagnation and deflationary pressures. Now often referred to as the "Lost Decades," Japan's economic growth has been relatively subdued compared to its rapid expansion in the post-war era.

While in the last couple of years Japan has been experiencing low inflation, one of the defining characteristics of Japan's economy has been its persistent struggle with deflation. Unlike the United States,

setagaya-has-the-largest-number-of-akiya-empty-homes-in-japan/

where inflation is a normal occurrence, Japan has faced prolonged periods of falling prices. Deflation has a detrimental impact on consumer spending and business investment, leading to a vicious cycle of reduced demand and sluggish economic growth.

In an attempt to combat deflation and boost economic activity, the Bank of Japan (BOJ) has pursued an ultra-accommodative monetary policy. Interest rates have been historically low for an extended period, with the BOJ adopting a near-zero or even negative interest rate policy. This has aimed to incentivize borrowing, spur investment, and increase spending. However, the effectiveness of such measures has been a subject of debate.

Since 2012 Japan has also embarked on a series of structural reforms under the banner of "Abenomics." Named after former Prime Minister Shinzo Abe, this policy framework aimed to promote economic growth through three arrows: monetary easing, fiscal stimulus, and structural reforms. While progress has been made, the country continues to face challenges in breaking free from deflationary pressures.

Depreciation

Now let's talk about depreciation. Unlike in many countries where houses and buildings appreciate in value, in Japan, buildings are subject to depreciation for tax purposes. The concept of depreciation allows the government to gradually reduce the assessed value of a building over time, reflecting its wear and tear and decreased value due to aging. The Japanese National Tax Agency provides a depreciation table that indicates the estimated useful life of different building structures. The table specifies the number of years over which the building's value is expected to decrease until it reaches a residual value of zero.

Here's an example of how depreciation works:

Let's say you own a wooden house, and the Japanese tax authorities have set the estimated useful life for wooden structures at twenty-two years. Each year, the value of your wooden house will decrease by a fixed percentage until it reaches zero after twenty-two years.

Suppose the initial value of your wooden house is ¥10,000,000 (~$69,000) excluding land. After the first year, if the depreciation rate is 5%, the assessed value for tax purposes will be ¥9,500,000 (¥10,000,000 - 5% of ¥10,000,000).

After the second year, the depreciation rate will be applied to the adjusted value of ¥9,500,000, resulting in a further decrease in value, and so on for the subsequent years until the estimated useful life of twenty-two years is reached.

The depreciation rate can vary depending on the building's structure and type. Tax laws and regulations also might be subject to change over time, so it's essential to consult with a tax professional or the local tax authorities for the most up-to-date and accurate information on building depreciation for tax purposes.

From my perspective, it's important to note that all akiyas (空き家), abandoned houses, I've encountered in Tokyo and it's surroundings have already reached a tax valuation of almost zero. Despite this low value, it's essential to remember that these properties are still houses, with the potential to be something more. While the tax valuation may show zero, I believe that with thoughtful investment and creative vision, these akiyas can become attractive homes for potential buyers or tenants. The key lies in leveraging the expertise of experienced real estate professionals who can assist in navigating the complexities of property renovations in Japan.

While the value of the actual houses on the land may depreciate, the land-value in popular areas tends to appreciate over time. The appreciation of land value in Japan is partly attributed to the limited land availability, particularly in urban centers like Tokyo. There can often be a stark contrast between the increasing value of the land and the decreasing value of older houses. If you want to access the land an old house stands on, you have to tear the old house down. This means that the "free house" you got when buying the land isn't really free. In reality it has a negative value. The overall cost of buying the property and removing the old house can be more than what the land and house are worth together.

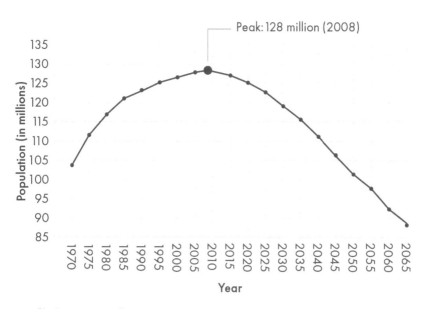

Declining Population in Japan

Declining Population

Japan's aging population and declining birth rates also pose significant challenges to its economic growth prospects. With the fastest-aging population of any post-industrial nation on earth, Japan's birth rate (the average number of children a woman has) started to decline in the 1970s, and in 2021 fell to 1.3. It takes a birth rate of about 2 to keep a steady population. In 2022 the population of Japan was 125.4 million people, having dropped by over a half-million people in one year. As a result, the workforce is shrinking, leading to a decrease in productivity and potential economic output. This demographic shift has far-reaching implications for various sectors, including the housing market.

JAPANESE PREFERENCE FOR NEW HOUSES

Not only are there fewer people in Japan, those people have a strong preference for newly-built properties. Japanese buyers prioritize modern amenities, advanced safety features, and the assurance of minimal maintenance. Newly-constructed properties are often considered a safer investment choice due to their lower risk of hidden defects and the potential for resale in the future.

Japanese homes are often built with a relatively shorter economic life in mind. Wooden structures are expected to be torn down in 20 years and concrete and steel buildings in 30 years. Due to the shorter expected life-span, often the building materials and techniques used in the past may not meet modern construction standards. As a result, older houses may require more frequent maintenance and renovation, further contributing to their depreciation.

Because of this, Japanese homeowners have a completely different relationship with their homes than Americans or Europeans. People aren't thinking about resale value because the house loses value rather than gains, and thus the house isn't maintained in order to increase its longevity. The house will have zero value eventually because of how the depreciation system works, plus it won't have the latest earthquake technology so it's not worth it. Because of this, the

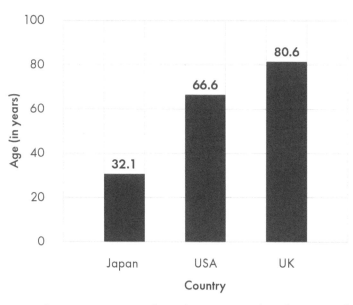

Average Age of Houses When Demolished

during the years 2008-2013

Japanese home owner just doesn't maintain their home in the same way as a US or European buyer would. Seasonal rituals designed to extend the life of your home that you may be used to in the US or Europe such as caulking exterior cracks, cleaning gutters or removing moss are not activities that Japanese homeowners participate in. There's simply no incentive to do so.

One of the interesting effects of this system I've noticed is that the rent for a brand-new house in Tokyo in some areas will be more than 40% higher than the rent for an apartment that is over thirty years old—even if they are in the same area, on the same street, or even right next to each other.

However, there are signs of a shift in this trend. Some homeowners are now exploring smaller-scale renovations, rethinking the

Aspects Japanese People
Care about When Looking for a Home

Aspect	Percentage
Rent	74.7%
Area	54.7%
Distance from train station	58.6%
Commuting time	57.8%
Layout	53.1%
Size	40.4%
Environment	49.6%
Move-in fees	34.0%
YEAR BUILT	38.6%
Appliances and fixtures	36.8%
Security	23.0%
Direction of house	17.4%
Number of rooms	20.0%
Proximity to parents	7.5%
Other	2.0%

idea of tearing down entire homes. Japan's changing demographics, including the declining and aging population, having led to a higher number of vacant homes, has prompted a new interest in rehabilitating older houses instead of building new ones. In particular, renovated manshons, similar to what an American would consider a condominium, are becoming more trendy. Additionally, in urban areas like Tokyo, innovative housing options are emerging. Companies are transforming old office spaces into apartments and creating co-living spaces, promoting a more affordable and communal way of living. This move away from traditional housing reflects the evolving needs and preferences of younger generations.

THE TREASURE TROVE

In the bustling heart of Tokyo, where ancient temples mingle with neon lights, lies a treasure trove. Through my journey of buying and renovating within this market, I've discovered countless opportunities, particularly in affordable Japanese houses. What I have found truly astonishing, especially in Tokyo, is the surprisingly low entry point. Properties that would be considered luxuries elsewhere are within reach here. Take, for instance, the Tree House apartment, which kickstarted my real estate journey. It's a prime example of how you can own a unique piece of Tokyo without breaking the bank.

While the Tree House wasn't technically an abandoned property, it was still priced at ¥14 million (~$96,500) for a 39 m^2 (420 ft^2) apartment only ten minutes from Shibuya Crossing. A new home in that same area that same size would be about ¥72.5 million (~$500,000). The Tree House was owned by a man who lived in Hiroshima. He hadn't come to Tokyo for years and didn't know what he wanted to do with it. There were so many old, cheap houses and he was competing to try and sell his. Many good real estate agents (called brokers in Japan) don't want to deal with selling them because the commissions are so low on such a low-priced property. The brokers simply don't put in much effort to sell the home. I'll share more about the purchase of the Tree House, and dealing with brokers, later in this book. The key point here is that there is a tremendous opportunity to find and renovate inexpensive homes in Japan, just like I have done many times.

Up until now, accessing information about this market, especially for non-Japanese speakers, has been quite challenging. That's precisely why sharing insights and experiences with a global audience is now more crucial than ever. I feel a strong sense of duty to debunk myths, demystify the complexities, and provide firsthand knowledge to an English-speaking audience. Akiya investments have become quite popular among Japanese investors in recent years, and there are already numerous books in Japanese on the subject. Here, I'm unlocking this world for the first time with an English-language book on the subject.

The intention of this book is to empower you with knowledge and ideas, not to provide specific financial recommendations. Please consult with a qualified financial professional before making any investment decisions.

I've heard your questions and curiosity, and I'm here to share. In this book, I'll pass on what I've learned from my own experiences, both good and bad, and from those of my friends. You'll gain a deep understanding of Tokyo's real estate market, especially when it comes to older Japanese houses, and the opportunities that lie within this growing market. By the end, you'll feel ready to confidently navigate this unique market.

But first, you'll have to get to Japan.

🔑 2

Planning Your Trip

In this chapter I'm going to share with you a list of things you should do to prepare yourself for living permanently in Japan, along with some of my own personal experiences. But the first thing I suggest you do is come visit Japan. Currently, US passport holders can stay in Japan as a tourist for 90 days as a "temporary visitor." The important thing is to get here and experience Japan, the culture, the food, the cities, and the people.

PLANNING FOR JAPAN

With a blend of timeless traditions and cutting-edge innovations, delicious cuisine, friendly faces, pristine streets, and beautiful vistas, Japan is an amazing country to explore. The cherry blossoms in spring and the changing leaves in autumn are sights to behold. Japan's four distinct seasons offer a variety of experiences, although be forewarned that the summer heat can be less inviting in Tokyo and beyond.

Knowing why you are coming to Japan, and what your plan is once you get here, will help guide the decisions you need to make and how you will prioritize your time. If you're considering buying property in Japan, it's vital to ask yourself why you're doing it. Are you seeking a permanent residence, an investment, or a unique experience? Your motivations will guide you through the intricate process of real estate acquisition here.

You should start by asking yourself this question: why are you interested in buying a house in Japan?

Because it's cheap or free?

Because you can?

Because you want to live in it?

Because you want to spend time in it?

Because it's an investment?

Because you like Japanese culture?

Because you have a sense of adventure, love renovation, and the thought of renovating a house in Japan makes you want to hop on a plane right now?

Whatever your reasons, it's important to spend some time asking yourself these questions so your motivations and goals are clear before embarking.

Now, let's dive into some things you should do to be well prepared.

LEARN THE LANGUAGE AND THE CULTURE

In hindsight I wish I had started studying Japanese earlier. No matter how dedicated you are, it will take time. Be consistent and study a little every day. If you're planning on moving to Japan in 2–3 years, start studying now and do at least thirty minutes a day.

While there are multiple ways to learn the language, I highly recommend immersing yourself by coming to Japan and spending time here. Get here, show respect for your surroundings and surround yourself with the language. If you can't be here, there are still ways to immerse yourself in the language. Watch Japanese movies. Go to Japanese restaurants. Read Japanese magazines, newspapers and books.

For me, when I decided to move I had about 3–4 months to prepare, and I considered myself a full time student of Japanese. I used every situation as an opportunity to learn. I studied two hours a day. I learned the Japanese symbols for the three writing systems: kanji, hiragana and katakana. I watched Japanese videos on YouTube and Japanese movies on Netflix. I read Japanese books and talked to Japanese friends online. This helped me get familiar with at least some of the culture and customs as well.

When I finally came to Japan permanently, I signed up for a language school in Shibuya, but quit a week later. It turned out that most people in the class were tourists just trying to get a Japanese visa and they were not serious about learning the language. They had all gotten scholarships to attend, planned to be there for a year, have fun, and then go back home, never to return. I had paid with my own money and was serious about learning Japanese. Here I was in a classroom filled with Spaniards and Italians who spent most of the time speaking to each other in their native languages. It was a waste of my time, and I decided I would learn better on my own.

I started taking classes online through italki.com, which worked perfectly for me. I was able to sit at home and get private tutoring, reading news, and talking about fun things with a real person, and it was only ¥1,450/hour ($10/hour) for someone good. You do need to search through and find the right person for you. I went through several teachers until I found the right one. But it's way more efficient than being in the language school. I paid less per hour getting private tutoring than I did in the language school classroom with twenty other people who weren't really interested in learning Japanese.

I also tried to make anything I was working on an opportunity to learn Japanese. For example, many models take acting classes—it helps with modeling, especially when doing commercial work, needing to portray a character for the client. So I decided to take a Japanese acting class.

I was the only foreigner in the school to have ever signed up for the long term class—no one there spoke English. I thought I knew Japanese customs, but the first day the other students told me off for not sitting up straight and listening to the teacher. I was listening, but because I wasn't sitting perfectly straight, they thought I wasn't. Then they told me off for not wearing slippers in the bathroom. In Japan, when you are in a school, an inn, or a home, there are special slippers that you use for the bathroom. You take off your street shoes at the door and put on your own indoor slippers. For the bathroom you take off your own slippers and wear special bathroom slippers. These aren't your own slippers, they are universal bathroom slippers by the bathroom door that are shared by everyone. The idea is that it is more hygienic since you are not tracking anything from the bathroom out into the home or school. Some people think it's kind of nasty wearing someone else's slippers, but it is culturally expected that you use the bathroom slippers. I knew about this but I was so nervous I simply forgot.

In the class I learned a lot about the Japanese language but also learned a lot about the culture. It is beautiful how they respect their teacher, it is like the teacher is a god. I learned about Japanese movies and how theater is made in Japan. I learned Japanese tongue twisters that took fifty hours for me to memorize and five full minutes to say. It was a great experience, but I'll never do it again.

When I started looking for houses, I made that a chance to learn Japanese as well. Searching real estate listings was partly about looking for a house and partly about seeing a word in the listing I didn't understand and learning what it meant. Six months later I was sitting with my broker signing the contract for my first home.

Jump in and experiment around until you find what works for you. You can find a lot of information about Japan online. Just know that you can find a lot of great advice, but a word of caution, you'll also find a lot of crappy advice as well. Use your common sense and check two or three different places before you decide something sounds right or not.

LEARN THE RULES

As you get within a few months of your trip to Japan, you're going to want to get squared away with necessities like visas, health insurance and other logistics for your stay.

Visas & Immigration

Owning a house or land in Japan doesn't automatically grant you citizenship, which makes sense. Citizenship involves more than a simple purchase and should reflect a deeper connection to the country. If it were that easy, anyone could become a Japanese citizen by just buying a cheap property.

How long you can stay in Japan on a given trip depends on what country you are a citizen of and which visa you are using or eligible for. If you aren't being brought here by work or business, then most likely you would be using a tourist visa or, for visitors from the US and some other countries, as a temporary visitor (no visa needed). Tourist visas (or temporary visitor status) are generally good for 90 days, but there's no clearly published answer as to whether you can use this type of visa multiple times a year or not. (Anecdotally, some say this is by design so Japanese authorities can have the flexibility to decide whether or not they want to let you back into the country or not.) The best advice is to work with a Japanese visa lawyer who can help you make sure you have the right information (and visa) for your situation.

The key point here is that it is (as far as I know) not possible to open a local Japanese bank account without a residency card or work visa. And purchasing a property without a local bank account, whether with cash or an international bank wire transfer, is possible, but financing can be challenging. Additionally, setting up a bank account for paying taxes and utilities might also be a challenge.

When I came to Japan, I was brought by my work here and my agency arranged a work visa for me. You may also qualify for a work visa, and for many people, a work visa longer than 6 months will automatically get you a residency card. There are also new "startup" visas that are a recent type of visa designed to attract foreign startup companies. You may also be able to get student visas by signing up for the Japanese language school (like the other students I met when I tried the school myself). Not the best way to learn Japanese, in my humble opinion, but worth it for the visa if you don't have another option.

For residents of some countries, there are also working holiday visas that allow a year-long working stay for visitors aged 18-30. Unfortunately, the United States is not one of the countries that is eligible for this program.

There are many options to look into, but remember it's crucial to obtain the right visa for your plans. For instance, if you arrive on a student visa, it's unlikely you can run a hotel business or an Airbnb under that visa. I was fortunate that my managers handled my visa arrangements during my initial contracts, allowing me to return to Japan easily.

Make sure your visa aligns with your intentions, and seeking advice from a lawyer is wise. I'm not a visa expert or a lawyer, but there are many lawyers specialized in helping foreigners get a valid visa in Japan, and I highly recommend you consult with one as you plan your trip.

While it's possible to visit Japan on a tourist visa or even purchase a house here as a foreigner without a working visa, be aware of Japan's rigorous immigration policies. If you're planning on staying permanently, your end goal is going to be to get a residency card. I personally believe these policies might become more lenient in the future, but that's just my speculation.

Health Insurance

Research Japan's healthcare system. While it's known for its high-quality care, understanding how it works, especially for non-residents, is critically important, especially if you have any ongoing health considerations, treatments, or medications you will need while you are here. You'll also want to make sure you understand what your health coverage will be and how it will work if you become sick or injure yourself while in Japan.

Telephone and Internet

The simplest solution to phone and internet is to make sure you have a good cell phone with a beefy data plan. It will take time (and some serious bureaucracy navigation skills) to get internet in any home or apartment you are in. I'll share more about the challenges of phone and internet in the next chapter, "Finding a Place to Live."

Banking

Be forewarned, because this is a biggie. You can't get a bank account without a residency card or a working visa. While you are here on a travel or tourist visa you will have to find a way to operate using your home country's banking system. It will be important to make sure you know how you will access your funds, which ATMs will work for you, and how to manage your accounts whether online or through international phone calls.

LEARN THE LANDSCAPE

Before your journey to Japan, take some time to familiarize yourself with the geography of Tokyo and Japan, and remember the most relevant or important places for your planned trip. Tokyo is the largest city in the world, but it's not one vast city. It is a collection of many smaller cities, with each subway station serving as the hub of its own little community.

One common misconception is that Tokyo Station is the center of Tokyo. To me, Shibuya Crossing (渋谷スクランブル交差点) is the center of Tokyo, and I never pass by Tokyo Station unless I have to go somewhere with the Shinkansen (新幹線), Japan's high-speed train, or "bullet train."

Research the local area you plan to stay or live in. Is there access to public transportation? What about hospitals, grocery stores, and other essential amenities? Are there convenience stores nearby? How far away is the closest subway and train station?

Street Names

There are no street names in Japan.

Imagine you're looking at a map of a city. Instead of seeing names for streets and areas, you see a grid with numbers. Each area, block, and building is assigned a specific number. Instead of saying "King's Street, Number 14 in New Town," you'd say "Building Number 4 in Block Number 5 within Area Number 2 in Shibuya." This numbering system is how Japanese addresses work and while it might seem unfamiliar at first, it becomes easier to understand with practice. Though, honestly, I still have a hard time with this when I am out on a casting because the buildings are not always numbered in order.

MAKE FRIENDS

Hopefully you've already picked up on the idea that making friends in Japan is going to be very important for your success here as a tourist, but most especially as a homebuyer. You've heard some of my adventures with Gavin, Norman, and others, and as we continue you are going to hear story after story of how the friends I have made in Japan have had a major influence in my being able to do what I am doing and do it successfully.

Community is key. I can't say it strongly enough.

Trust me. Make friends. With neighbors, with co-workers (if you have them), with other expats, with professionals. You will be so glad that you did.

MAKE A PLAN

Okay! You've researched, you've learned, you've networked, you've daydreamed, and you've brainstormed. Now it's time to get concrete. It's time to start planning.

Your Stuff

This is going to come up over and over again, but in case you didn't already know it—there's not a lot of space in Japan. Everything there is small, so much smaller than what you're most likely used to, especially if you live in the US. You need to start preparing, right now, to bring, or possibly even keep, *very few* things. When I came to Japan I came with just my suitcase, as I did for all of my modeling jobs. Some of the models actually had an ongoing competition to see who could travel with the least amount of things. My friend Charlie actually went to Paris to work for fashion week with nothing but the clothes he was wearing, his wallet and his phone. I don't recommend spending an entire week in the heat of summer in the same pair of underwear, but he did win the bet.

You don't have to go that far, but you do want to seriously consider what you bring. Anything you could possibly want you can buy here, and your electronics probably won't work here anyway, so other than a few clothes and your personal items, you really don't need anything. Things that you no longer need can be sold, donated or given to friends and family. If you have a few precious things that you know you will want to keep for later, but it doesn't make sense to bring them while you're still traveling back and forth, look at what storage options there are. I had the luxury of being able to leave those things at my Mom's house in Sweden when I was still looking for my permanent home.

If you decide to come to Japan permanently, again, you will not want to pay to ship things unless they are too precious to part with. And anything you leave at home will have to be dealt with and that will cost time and money when you'll want to be focused on getting back here. So take the time now and pare down. Look at everything you have and ask yourself. Do I really need this in Japan? Is it going to be worth the freight cost, the headache and the stress to ship it there? Once it's there will I have space for it in Japan's smaller living spaces?

Everyone has to make their own decisions, but try to be detached. Remember: you are going to be embarking on an adventure that few people go on. Don't let your future be bogged down by your stuff.

Your Budget

One of the things you will need to consider when planning both your initial travel to Japan and your eventual relocation here is how much money you have to work with. How much is it going to cost you to travel? How are you going to stay afloat while you are here? Will you be working remotely? Will you have bills to cover back home? Where will you be staying until your home is bought, renovated and ready to live in or rent? How much will that cost? Consider all of the possible expenses you might have and how you will cover them. Don't forget to include a buffer for unexpected expenses or emergencies.

Once you are ready to purchase and renovate a home, what will your budget be? Will you have to use financing to purchase your house? Research financing options in Japan for foreigners. Some banks might be hesitant to loan money to non-residents or those without permanent residency status. In addition to the base costs for both purchasing and renovating, be aware that there are many fees and taxes you will be responsible for—we'll talk more about that in upcoming chapters.

Another thing to consider in this category is the long-term plan for your renovated home. Will you stay in Japan or move on to a new country or go back home? Think about what you might want or need to do with the home you have renovated in that case. Will you resell it? Rent it? Consider the financial implications of all of those choices.

All the Rest

Of course there's as many things to plan as there are people doing the planning. Everyone's individual situation, goals and resources will be different. Have a good brainstorming session, maybe with a friend or partner, and try to figure out as much as you can. Whatever else you have to figure out, some things you'll definitely want to include will be your travel arrangements, your timeline, and your personal needs such as medical care or other treatments, medications or therapies. Leave no stone unturned so that your adventure will be as comfortable and worry-free as possible!

YOU'RE ON YOUR WAY

Whew! That's a lot of planning. But now you're well prepared to take the first step on this incredible journey. Once you arrive in Japan, you'll have so many things to do and see and experience, but one thing you'll probably want to do is find somewhere longer-term to stay. We'll cover that in the next chapter.

COUNTDOWN TO JAPAN

12 Months Before

- **Cultural Understanding:** Explore Japanese customs and etiquette through online resources or local classes.
- **Language:** Start learning Japanese. You can start with an app like Duolingo or Rosetta Stone, but look into italki.com for conversational learning.
- Research: Learn about abandoned homes (akiyas) in Japan and how to find, buy and renovate them. (That's what this book is for!)

9 Months Before

- **Visas & Legalities:** Start your visa research. Understand the different types of visas available and what you're eligible for.
- **Budget:** Put a tentative budget in place. Consider costs like travel, living expenses, the property, renovation, and emergencies.
- **Packing, Part 1:** Decide which belongings to sell, store or ship. Begin selling or donating what you don't need and research shipping and storage for the rest.

6 Months Before

- **Local Contacts:** Start making connections through forums, expat groups, and social media.

- **Healthcare:** Research vaccinations, health precautions and healthcare systems for Japan. Consider a comprehensive check-up. Plan for ongoing medication or treatment needs.
- **Emergency Preparedness:** Familiarize yourself with Japan's natural disaster guidelines for the area you will be in. Plan an appropriate emergency kit.

3 Months Before

- **Visas:** Initiate the visa application process if you haven't already.
- **Local Infrastructure & Amenities:** Narrow down your options for accommodations and consider proximity to public transport, hospitals, and grocery/ convenience stores. Plan for phone and/or internet service.
- **Research Professionals:** Make a list of real estate brokers or consultants familiar with the akiya market. (Don't bother contacting them until you are there in person—we'll talk about this later.)

1 Month Before

- **Packing, Part 2:** Start packing for your trip. Arrange for shipping for any large items you need to take with you.

- **Insurance:** Look into both travel and property insurance. You will need both. I get mine through my credit card company.
- **Financial Preparations:** Make sure you know how to access your funds from Japan. Know the transfer options and current currency conversion rates.

2 Weeks Before: The Final Countdown

- **Confirmations:** Double-check all bookings, flights and accommodations.
- **Medical Preparations:** Get any needed last-minute health check-ups or vaccinations.
- **Learning:** Continue studying Japanese language and culture. This will continue for years, even after you live here.

A Few Days Before

- **Packing:** Finalize your packing. Ensure you have all essential documents, chargers, and any immediate necessities.
- **Goodbyes:** Spend time with loved ones. Consider hosting a farewell gathering.
- **Take a Moment:** You are about to embark on the adventure of a lifetime! Enjoy it. Savor it.

🔑 3

Finding a Place to Live

After having lived in many major metropolises around the world, I feel safe to say that Tokyo's rental market stands out as the most intricate and complex. Navigating this complicated system requires understanding fees, customs, and unique practices that can be quite bewildering for newcomers, and even for some Japanese locals.

The process of renting an apartment in Tokyo usually includes substantial upfront costs including key money, deposits, and various fees, which usually are significantly higher than the monthly rent itself. These practices have historical roots and can be a burden for many renters.

While Tokyo's real estate landscape is gradually evolving, it is important for both prospective tenants and property owners to remain well-informed and work with trusted brokers. Let's dive into the Japanese rental market so you can find a place to live while you're looking for your first house renovation project.

EXPLORING HOUSING OPTIONS

You're fresh off the plane and ready to embark on your new adventure. On your first trip (or two, or five) you are likely going to be on a tourist visa, which limits your stay to 90 days. That's a good thing, because you need time to get to know the country and the various areas before you make a longer commitment. Before settling into a long-term rental, or later, your renovated home, you'll need to start with a short-term rental while you explore the housing market in Tokyo.

Short-term accommodations, such as serviced apartments or guesthouses, are popular options, and of course you can also stay in an Airbnb, such as my Sangenjaya House. Another popular option is a share house, similar to the one featured on the Netflix show Terrace House. This is what I stayed in when I first moved to Japan. A share house is simply a home in which people rent the individual bedrooms, but share the kitchen and other common areas. Kind of like living with roommates except that everyone who lives there has made their arrangements separately with the owner and likely do not know each other. These communal living spaces foster a sense of community and provide an excellent opportunity to make friends and build connections with people from diverse backgrounds. You can find listings for share houses on popular platforms like Facebook groups and Craigslist. Some brokers also deal with share house rentals.

The advantages of share houses lie in their convenience. Most share houses come fully furnished, saving tenants the hassle and cost of buying furniture. Additionally, utilities and internet fees are typically included in the rent, simplifying monthly budgeting. For those new to Japan or looking for a more sociable living arrangement, share houses are a great option.

Furnished apartments provide an enticing option for those seeking a more straightforward relocation process. These apartments come fully equipped with furniture, appliances, and essential household items, allowing tenants to move in with just their personal belongings. Such convenience is especially attractive for short-term stays or those who prefer a hassle-free transition. Craigslist is a good place to find a furnished apartment.

While the initial costs of renting a furnished apartment might be lower due to the absence of upfront furniture expenses, it's essential to be aware that the monthly rent can be significantly higher compared to unfurnished units. The added convenience and flexibility come at a premium, making furnished apartments a suitable choice for those willing to pay extra for comfort and ease.

All of these options, Airbnb, share houses, and furnished apartments, offer convenience and flexibility, allowing you to adjust to the city without rushing into a long-term commitment. The plus? Initial costs are low. And the minus? The monthly rent is salted! (That's a Swedish expression that means more expensive.) It's a cost versus convenience balance and you'll need to decide what balance works for you.

While staying in your short-term rental, take advantage of this time to research different neighborhoods and their amenities. Consider factors like proximity to your workplace (assuming you are working), access to public transportation, and the overall vibe of the area. Each Tokyo neighborhood has its own unique charm, so finding the one that suits your lifestyle is essential.

Having narrowed down the areas you want to start looking for a long-term rental, it's important to understand the types of housing options there are, and what they are called. After five years of living in Japan and speaking fluent Japanese, I still find myself grappling with the language nuances when it comes to housing terminology. In particular, the word "apartment" has different connotations in Japanese culture, often associated with student housing or smaller living spaces.

On the other hand, the term "manshon" can be misleading. My own cozy 39 m2 (420 ft2) apartment, which I fondly call my "Tree House," is a manshon apartment, but doesn't fit the luxurious image that word may evoke. In Japan, manshon (マンション) refers to a multi-story building where individual units are often owned rather than rented. Though it may not be a grand mansion, I pay monthly management and common area fees and require permission for any renovations or improvements, similar to a condominium in the United States.

DIFFERENT BUILDING TYPES

Apaatos

An apaato (アパート), a loan-word from English based on "apartment," is the cheapest form of rental housing in Japan. It is usually a very small, wood-built building with little-to-no sound-proofing that tends to be preferred by students and other residents who may not be staying long-term. They offer a range of advantages and disadvantages that cater to different needs and preferences of residents. These two-story buildings are divided into multiple small apartments, upstairs and downstairs. While never fancy, apaatos are often preferred for their affordability, compact living spaces, smaller building size, and fewer residents, as compared to larger apartment complexes. Additionally, some apaatos are standalone houses, providing a more individual living experience.

One of the key advantages of living in an apaato is its cost-effectiveness, while one of the disadvantages is the potential lack of insulation, which can lead to cold rooms and sound insulation problems. This lack of acoustic privacy can be reminiscent of scenes from Japanese manga, where characters are often portrayed living in apaatos with thin walls that allow them to hear their neighbors' every move. While this might add some charm to the manga storylines, in reality, it can be less than ideal for you in seeking a peaceful and secluded living space.

Manshons

Manshon (マンション) is a bigger apartment building, or what most Westerners would consider condominiums, where they are often owned and not rented. These are multi-story buildings, often up to 7–8 stories tall, that are better quality buildings typically constructed using high-quality steel-reinforced concrete (SRC). For example, the Tree House is in a building four stories tall with sixteen apartments. My apartment is located on the third and fourth floors, with the main apartment on the third floor and a loft on the fourth.

In Japanese cities, you can find a variety of manshon buildings, ranging from at least three floors high to towering skyscrapers, known as tawaamanshon (タワーマンション). Tawaamanshon, which are over ten floors high, are abundant in major cities, as they are considered prestigious and attractive to many Japanese residents.

Manshons are keylocked buildings, often with bike storage, sometimes a doorman, and often a management company maintaining the building. Units are often a mixture of being owned and rented. There are management fees for upkeep of the building and you have to receive permission for any renovations.

In many manshon buildings, residents own their units, leading to more long-term residents who prioritize good relationships with their neighbors. They offer a quieter and more convenient living experience but may come with additional responsibilities required by building management.

Free-Standing Houses

Another good option, if available in the neighborhood you want to be in, is an ikkodate （戸建て）, or free-standing house (detached house). You may also see the terms chuukou ikkodate （中古 一戸建て）, a used house, and shinchiku ikkodate （新築 一戸建て） a newly built free-standing house. Renting a free-standing house gets you involved in the neighborhood, and you gain the experience of what Japanese homes are like. There are many affordable homes available to rent to foreigners. I have two friends who specialize in renovating homes especially for foreigners, single mothers, and other people who might usually have a harder time renting. You can learn about them in the "Exploring Investment Strategies" chapter. In general, when looking for a long-term rental situation in a free-standing house (or later a house to buy), I recommend suumo.jp or just walking inside the local brokerage in the area you are looking for a place to stay.

SETTING A BUDGET

You'll want to set a budget for your rental expenses, considering not just the monthly rent but also the initial costs like gratitude money, deposit, and agency fees. You'll need to prepare necessary documents such as a valid visa, proof of employment or income, and a Japanese phone number, as landlords may require them during the application process. In most cases you'll need a Japanese residency card.

UNDERSTANDING ALL THE FEES

Before I started my YouTube channel, Anton in Japan, earlier this year (2023), I had been doing YouTube in Japanese for a national audience. I had about 100,000,000 views, and was doing content about DIY, home renovation and the cultural differences of Japan compared to the rest of the world. One of my most viewed videos on this channel is about how stupid I think the system of gratitude money is. My thought has always been: "When renting an apartment here in Japan why can't they just bake in this money within the rent?" Raise the rent by 5–10% instead of fooling people into thinking the rent is cheap. I can understand a deposit, but this fee is outrageous.

"Introducing Netflix 7.1X Plus! With our subscription, you can experience the ultimate in streaming entertainment. For a sign-up fee that's six times your monthly cost, you'll gain access to a world of binge-worthy shows and movies. But that's not all—every two years, we'll treat you to the exciting opportunity to renew your viewing experience with an additional exorbitant fee."

Would you sign up for this deal? This is how the Japanese rental market often works in Tokyo.

Gratitude Money

"Gratitude money, what's that?" you're probably asking. In Japanese gratitude money, or key money, is called reikin (礼金). Rei means gratitude, and kin means money. Gratitude money is essentially a bribe paid to your landlord, a gift from you to him, for letting you rent his property. Some people believe that this is a holdover from the Great Kantō Earthquake in 1923. After the earthquake there wasn't enough housing and people were grateful to landlords for a place to stay so they would give them a gift of gratitude money. This reikin could be an amount from 1–3 times the monthly rent. "Thank you for letting me pay money to live in your apartment you're already making money from by renting to me." In some cases, you may be able to negotiate this fee away, and older apartments usually don't have these fees, making them a more budget-friendly option for some tenants.

Security Deposit

In Japan, when renting an apartment, tenants pay a security deposit called shikikin (敷金). It's like a safety payment for landlords in case of any damage or unpaid rent, similar to many other countries where security deposits are common. The amount and rules can vary, so it's essential to understand local regulations. The deposit is usually refundable when you move out—if there's no damage. Remember to communicate with your landlord and document the property's condition to ensure a smooth refund process.

Renewal Fee

The renewal fee, koushin-ryou (更新料), is usually paid every second year to renew your contract. Typically, about one month's rent.

Agent Fee

The agent fee, or chukai tesuryou (仲介手数料), is a one-time payment to the real estate broker for their services in helping you find and secure a rental property. The agent fee is usually equivalent to one month's rent (plus tax) and is paid upon signing the lease agreement. It covers the broker's work in showing you available properties, negotiating with landlords, and preparing the necessary paperwork. The owner also pays one month of rent to the broker for this service.

Guarantor Fee

In some cases, landlords may require you to have a guarantor, especially if you are a foreigner or don't meet specific income requirements. A guarantor is someone who will take responsibility for your rent if you are unable to pay. If you don't have a personal guarantor, you can use the services of a guarantor company, and they will charge you a guarantor fee, called hoshou gaisha tesuryou (保証会社手数料). The guarantor fee is typically around half to one month's rent (plus tax) and is paid to the guarantor company.

Maintenance Fee

The maintenance fee, kyouekihi (共益費), is common in apartment (manshon) buildings and covers shared expenses like cleaning and maintenance of common areas. It can vary depending on the building. If there is one it's usually not more than ¥14500 ($100), but if you rent a more luxurious and expensive place, it can be higher.

Fire Insurance

It's mandatory to have fire insurance, kasai hoken (火災保険), when renting a property. The cost can vary but is usually around ¥20,000 to ¥30,000 per year (~$135–$210).

Initial Cleaning Fee

This is a one-time payment for cleaning the property before you move in. This initial cleaning fee, shoki seisou hi (初期清掃費), usually costs about ¥30,000–¥100,000 (~$200–$690) but can sometimes cost more depending on the size of your apartment.

Lock Exchange Fee

The lock exchange fee, jou koukan hi (錠交換費), ensures that you have a new set of keys and enhances security by preventing previous tenants from accessing the property. The exact cost may vary depending on the landlord or the real estate company handling the property. Usually a one-time payment of around ¥10,000–¥30,000 (~$70–$210).

Moving Company Fee

If you hire a moving company to help with your move, they will charge you a moving company fee: hikkoshi hiyou (引越し費用).

EXAMPLE OF RENTAL FEES

Now that we've looked at all the various fees, let's look at an example. Assuming a monthly rent of ¥100,000 (~$690) for a small apartment in Tokyo, here's a simplified breakdown of the potential costs involved:

Initial Move-in Expenses

Security Deposit:	¥100,000 ($690)
Gratitude Money:	¥200,000 ($1,380)
First Month's Rent:	¥100,000 ($690)
Subtotal:	¥400,000 ($2,760)

Fees

Brokerage Fee:	¥110,000 ($760)
Guarantee Fee:	¥50,000 ($345)
Fire Insurance:	¥20,000 ($140)
Key Replacement:	¥30,000 ($205)
Subtotal:	¥210,000 ($1,450)

TOTAL: **¥610,000 ($4,210)**

You've now paid a total of ¥610,000 ($4,210) in order to move in, over six times your annual monthly rent of ¥100,000 ($690). You'll also have some expenses that are paid annually, like household fire insurance of around ¥20,000 ($138), and the annual guarantor fee renewal of approximately ¥10,000 ($69). Plus, every two years you'll have a renewal fee ranging from ¥50,000 ($345) up to ¥100,000 ($690).

Please remember that these are rough estimates and the actual costs can differ based on various factors. The example here was designed to give you an idea of the intricacies of understanding the rental market in Tokyo, and understanding the high cost of the move-in and renewal fees.

YOU'LL PROBABLY NEVER GET YOUR DEPOSIT FEES BACK

When I was looking for rentals in New York or Stockholm, we had a housing crisis, and no landlord ever had to care about tiny small pinholes in the walls. It's not really clean? Everything isn't working? There's bedbugs? No problem—we are ready to rent this place out.

Not so in Tokyo. Tenants have an expectation that the place should look *New*. New cushion flooring (vinyl flooring) and new white wallpaper. **New** is good in Japan, and you will be financially responsible for making it look **New** for the future tenant. The owner most likely will keep your deposit fees to redo the surfaces, wallpaper and flooring, to make the place look **New** again. That is what people expect.

If there is one dent in the floor, the owner will put new flooring in the entire apartment. If there is one hole in the wallpaper they will put new wallpaper in the entire apartment. I had a friend that had used a pushpin to hang a single photo of far-away loved ones in his rented apartment. The landlord charged him thousands of dollars to re-wallpaper the entire apartment. Needless to say, my friend didn't get his deposit back.

RENTAL STICKER SHOCK

The upfront costs for renting an apartment in Tokyo are nothing short of jaw-dropping, and the fact that a significant portion of this money won't find its way back to your pocket is absurd. Just take a look at the math—a whopping ¥610,000 ($4,210) before even stepping foot into your new place. That's not even considering the potential expense of hiring a moving company on top of it all. You're essentially forking out over six times your monthly rent just to secure a place to live. It's like paying for a privilege you might never fully enjoy. And the cherry on top? Once you're through this financial obstacle course, the relentless rent payments begin.

Let's be honest here—some folks in the real estate game are intentionally muddying the waters. They're crafting a bewildering web of fees, charges, and costs, leaving you scratching your head wondering where your hard-earned cash is vanishing to. It's like they've invented a special language of their own, designed to keep you in the dark and your wallet perpetually open.

This whole setup begs the question: is this complexity a deliberate ploy to keep renters in the dark about their own money? It certainly seems that way. While you're left grappling with numbers that don't make sense and fees that seem to appear out of thin air, they're probably enjoying a good laugh all the way to the bank. (And yes, successful friends of mine working in bigger real estate corporations have confirmed this.)

There's one good way to look at the fees: they're motivating! These fees were a driving factor in my decision to buy my Tree House apartment. Guess what? The entire process cost me just ¥500,000 ($3,450) in fees to buy a manshon apartment close to Shibuya Crossing, the biggest and busiest street crossing in the world.

SECURING A LONG-TERM RENTAL

While you can look for rentals online on portals like Suumo and Athome,* you will need an agent in the end to physically go have a look at the place. Japan still operates in many analog ways, and in most cases, the brokers have rental properties that haven't even reached the online market yet. Working with them not only streamlines the process but also opens up opportunities for off-market deals.

Navigating the rental market in Tokyo can be challenging, especially if you're not fluent in Japanese. Consider seeking assistance from a bilingual broker or a housing agency specializing in serving foreigners. They can guide you through the process, help you find suitable options, and translate the lease agreements for you. With the help of your broker, schedule property viewings based on your

---

* You'll find the links in the "More Information" chapter at the end of the book.

🔑

RENTAL TIPS FROM AN EXPERT

Erik Nasriddinov: E-Housing at e-housing.jp

I had the honor of sitting down with Erik Nasriddinov, the CEO of E-Housing and a prominent figure in Tokyo's bustling Real Estate scene. He assists hundreds of clients each year in navigating the challenging housing market to find their ideal place to call home in central Tokyo.

E-Housing Tokyo's core focus is aiding expats and newcomers in Japan in their housing journey. They specialize in facilitating short and long-term rentals, along with supporting foreigners interested in property purchases within Tokyo's central seven wards. Foreigners often find the quality of life in Tokyo surprisingly affordable. From remarkable food options to Michelin-star restaurants, Tokyo's offerings often come at a fraction of the cost compared to other major cities.

The primary hurdle for foreigners seeking accommodation in Tokyo is the market's lack of transparency. Online listings are often misleading, with up to 30–40% being available due to outdated information and unverified brokers. E-Housing concentrates on neighborhoods like Setagaya, Shibuya, Meguro, Minato, Shinjuku, Shinagawa, and Chuo ku, which are particularly accommodating to both Japanese and foreign residents.

A common misconception is that time is abundant for decision-making. In reality, desirable properties rent out swiftly, especially in the ¥290,000 ($2,000) to ¥725,000 ($5,000) range.

Erik's advice to newcomers is to actively search to find the right property. Trusting agents completely might lead to mismatched expectations. One should start searching around six weeks in advance and personally visiting the properties is crucial to getting the best outcome.

Expats typically prioritize features like spacious outdoor areas, gyms, and swimming pools. In contrast, Japanese nationals tend to focus more on interior design and the age of the building. Certain properties may restrict foreigners due to cultural differences and tenant-friendly laws. Owners seek trustworthy tenants they can effectively communicate with, as exemplified by Japan's stringent trash disposal rules.

Erik believes the housing market is poised to evolve with the influx of foreigners. Technology-driven solutions are crucial as Japanese systems are complex. A recent legal change allowing digital rental agreements signals a shift toward online processes. Landlords are becoming more open to renting to foreigners and easing restrictions, especially in newer buildings.

Note: You'll find Erik Nasriddinov's contact info in the "More Information" chapter at the end of the book.

preferences and budget. Be open to various housing options, from traditional Japanese apartments (manshons) to modern high-rise buildings. Take note of the apartment's condition, amenities, and proximity to public facilities like subways, schools, supermarkets, hospitals, and convenience stores.

Work with a broker you trust and ask a lot of questions. Be clear about your budget and the area you want to live. Don't want to pay ridiculous moving-in fees? Tell your broker, he might be able to negotiate on your behalf. Make sure you take videos and photos of the place before you move in, you don't want to be charged for something ridiculous when moving out again.

Once you've found your ideal place, you'll need to submit a rental application. The landlord will review your documents and may require a guarantor or a co-signer if you don't meet certain criteria. Once approved, you'll sign the lease agreement and pay the necessary (and outrageous!) fees and deposits.

Congratulations! You've secured your new Tokyo home. Upon moving in, take care of any required registrations, such as notifying the local municipality about your new address. Set up utilities, like electricity, water, and internet, and familiarize yourself with the building's rules and waste disposal system.

GETTING PHONE & INTERNET

Through my time in Japan I've realized that foreigners face an even bigger challenge when renting apartments: dealing with Japanese bureaucracy. This can be especially daunting for newcomers to Tokyo. Renting an apartment here can feel like a cat-and-mouse game. To rent, you need a phone number and a bank account, but to get those, you need a permanent address, which, in turn, requires a bank account. However, opening a bank account often demands a phone number. It's a frustrating loop that can send you bouncing between your broker, phone provider, and bank until everything finally aligns. This is another reason why working with a local broker or service can help you know how to get everything sorted.

I've often been asked about how internet connections work in Japan. While my mobile provider, Rakuten, offers excellent unlimited internet for my phone, the signal can get shaky during rainy days. It's a mystery. If you are renting a manshon or free-standing home that is new or renovated there is likely internet service installed and you would just need to contact the provider to set up an account. Ask the landlord for information! Once you buy your home, you will most likely need to have new wires installed during your renovation to get internet service. I'd recommend doing this during promotional campaigns or bundling your phone and internet services into one contract to potentially save money and get priority service.

The process of getting new wires installed can be a bit cumbersome, and wait times can be lengthy, even in central Tokyo. I recall waiting for over two months for a technician to come and install the wires in my first house. Additionally, there's usually a fee of around ¥45,000 ($310), and they might offer you a router, but only if you commit to a two-year contract.

Surprisingly, it can be easier to buy a house in Japan than to sign up for phone or internet service if you're not a resident. It's like they're saying, "Sure, you can have a house, but good luck streaming your favorite shows or calling your friends!" The paperwork and requirements for phone and internet contracts can sometimes feel like you're trying to crack a secret code, while buying a house might seem like a walk in the park by comparison. So, if you're a non-resident planning to tackle this bureaucratic adventure, bring your patience and a sense of humor—you might need both!

TIME TO EMBRACE THE TOKYO LIFESTYLE

Now that you're settled into your new Tokyo home, it's time to embrace the city's vibrant lifestyle. Explore the neighborhoods, indulge in the delicious local cuisine, have a Strong Zero from your local convenience store and immerse yourself in the rich culture and traditions Japan has to offer.

While you're exploring Tokyo, it's also time to explore the investment opportunities that await. We'll cover those in detail in the next chapter. See you there!

Part 2
ACQUIRING

🗝 4

Exploring Investment Strategies

In the heart of Tokyo's vibrant Yutenji（祐天寺）neighborhood, just a short hop away from Nakameguro（中目黒）, a unique and unexpected opportunity unfolded before my eyes. It all began when I met a Japanese woman in her 50s, named Kyoko, who owned an old building. Her son, a friend of mine, had been trying to introduce us for some time, and I finally agreed to meet her.

Now, if you're not familiar with Yutenji or Nakameguro, let me give you a quick snapshot. Nakameguro boasts the world's largest Starbucks, which opened in 2019, and is famous for its stunning cherry blossoms in the spring. It's a welcoming place for foreigners, with an array of great restaurants, bars, and izakayas（居酒屋）, Japanese pubs. One of the standout spots is Barry's, a bar located in an old factory building where you can even play ping pong. Yutenji, right next door, has a more residential feel, but it comes with sky-high real estate prices, making even a small piece of land cost a million dollars.

I agreed to meet Kyoko, and before our meeting, she showed me some pictures of her building. To my surprise, it was more like a castle than a regular building. As I arrived, I was greeted by a massive, architect-designed wall that looked like an optician's lens and plenty of parking space—even a garage. It was one of those mysterious facades that make you wonder what's hidden inside.

Once inside, Kyoko and her son led me through a house filled with grandeur. The first two rooms were enormous, with high ceilings, pianos, golden wallpaper, and chandeliers, giving off a distinctly French vibe. But the real eye-opener was the sprawling, somewhat neglected but once-beautiful Japanese garden at the back.

Amid all the antiques, paintings, and personal belongings, Kyoko shared her dilemma. She wanted to restore this magnificent 50-year-old, 300 m^2 (3,229 ft^2) house built by a Japanese architect at her successful businessman father's request. The property, covering around 800 m^2 (8,611 ft^2) is estimated to be worth about ¥1.5 billion (~$10,350,000) due to its prime location.

Here's the twist—every company Kyoko consulted with advised her to tear it down, which was the last thing she wanted to do. Despite her desire for renovation, they only saw the property's land value. They couldn't see the potential in the house, even though it only needed some maintenance and updates. A "paint and paper" job as we say in DIY.

Kyoko turned to me because she knew of my passion for renovating and reviving old homes. She implored, "Anton, can you help me preserve my beloved house? Could you turn it into an Airbnb or a shooting location? Please, use my house and make it beautiful again."

As I left the house, I couldn't help but wonder if I could take on such a massive project. What would I do with this magnificent property? This wasn't a fictional story; it was a real-life puzzle. The house, with its incredible garden, was a hidden gem, waiting to be brought back to its former glory.

Indeed, it's a remarkable situation, and it reflects a common dilemma in a country like Japan, where the threat of earthquakes has driven a tear-down-and-rebuild culture. However, it's also a testament to the deep emotional connection people can have with their homes, one that often transcends financial considerations. Kyoko's unwavering love and attachment to her family's house, despite the prevailing trends, demonstrates the profound value we place on the places we call home. It's a reminder that there are stories and emotions woven into the walls of our dwellings that can't be measured in terms of money alone.

MULTIPLE INVESTMENT STRATEGIES

There are multiple investment strategies that can create substantial returns, with remarkably low buy-in points, especially when it comes to older properties by Japanese standards. Below I'll share a collection of stories, insights and investment strategies from my own experiences, and from passionate real estate enthusiasts I've met here in Japan. There are several distinct paths to success that showcase the remarkable potential of the Japanese real estate market.

STRATEGY: CENTRALLY LOCATED AIRBNB

How it works: find and buy an abandoned house in a central urban area, renovate it, and turn it into an Airbnb.

I love finding old properties in central Tokyo and turning them into unique gems. My Sangenjaya House is a perfect example of this where I mixed Scandinavian and Japanese architecture in one, old Japanese house.

This strategy works by buying an abandoned house in a central urban area, then renovating it and turning it into an Airbnb. Having a house for short-term rentals provides more freedom and flexibility compared to apartments, which often have strict regulations for obtaining Airbnb licenses. With my Sangenjaya House, I've been able to avoid those hassles and offer travelers an exceptional experience. For various reasons, Japanese tenants and buyers usually prioritize newly-built over anything else, and what you are looking for and what is trendy in your country and within your culture, is probably not that popular among Japanese renters or buyers. This makes the Japanese market hot for foreign buyers, since we see beauty and opportunities in something that might be neglected and not considered beautiful in the local market.

It's not always easy to locate these neglected properties, and some detective work is often needed to find the owners. But the effort is worth it. These houses often can't be rebuilt due to narrow roads, so they're not in demand among regular homebuyers. That means we don't have to compete with them, and we can get them at affordable prices with investment loans or cash purchases.

I poured my heart and soul into the renovation of my Sangenjaya House, and the results have been remarkable. The house has garnered attention on social media and has become a popular choice on Airbnb. The returns on this investment have been truly outstanding, granting me the financial flexibility to delve into content creation and explore even more captivating renovation ventures

ahead. Furthermore, I have the privilege of hosting wonderful guests who delight in experiencing a unique, spacious standalone house in Tokyo.

Sharing my journey through the *Tokyo Renovation Diaries* series on my YouTube channel, *Anton in Japan*, has allowed me to inspire others and showcase the beauty of these unique properties. I'm proud to have found a path that combines my passion for renovation with an enriching and profitable venture in the dynamic Japanese real estate market, while encouraging others to do the same.

🔑

If you are considering a renovation project, a chuukou ikkodate (中古 一戸建て), an old or used free-standing house, can be more straightforward to deal with in terms of making renovations and simple home improvements. Unlike buying a brand new property, purchasing an chuukou ikkodate often allows homeowners to make changes without needing to seek extensive permission or adhere to strict regulations. This greater freedom in the renovation process can be appealing to those looking to personalize and revitalize their home without facing unnecessary bureaucratic hurdles. Additionally, renovating a chuuko ikkodate offers a unique opportunity to preserve the charm of traditional Japanese architecture while infusing it with modern comforts and aesthetics.

By transforming abandoned houses into vibrant living spaces, we are not only generating remarkable returns on investment but also solving a societal problem. Neighbors often express their gratitude, as these renovated properties eliminate fire hazards and contribute to the betterment of the entire neighborhood.

So, with dedication, tenacity, and a passion for renovation, transforming neglected houses into lucrative Airbnb rentals can be an exciting and fulfilling endeavor. Embracing the allure of these extraordinary spaces has allowed me to leave a lasting impression on travelers and make a significant impact on the Japanese real estate landscape.

STRATEGY: VACATION AIRBNB

How it works: find and buy an abandoned house in a tourist area, renovate it so it looks fresh, clean and new, and do vacation rentals to Japanese vacationers.

My friend Ken, a Filipino-Japanese man, moved to Japan when he was 10-years old. He works in recruiting specializing in executive management roles in Tokyo.

Ken's journey into real estate began seven years ago when he bought his first property in Tokyo that he turned into a share house. Two years ago, he took a bold step and got an abandoned four-bedroom house next to the ocean in Kamogawa (鴨川市), Chiba (千葉県). The site was a complete mess, a literal bamboo jungle. He found it online, saw it in person, and made an offer the same day. The seller accepted.

Ken spent about four months renovating the house, clearing out the garden, building a deck, and acquiring a hotel license. He now rents it to people who love to BBQ and enjoy the ocean views.

This was Ken's first short-term rental property but he still made all his money back in less than a year. "When I don't have guests, I enjoy spending my own time here," he says. He used the profits to buy another property, this time in Atami (熱海市), famous for its hot springs, fireworks, and easy access from Tokyo via the Shinkansen (新幹線), the high-speed train.

The neighbors are very happy the house is now being used, and Ken is on good terms with them. Ken pays one of the neighbors, who is a fisherman, to help out with garbage and other small things to maintain the property, which is a win-win for both of them.

Much like me, Ken is always seeking fresh challenges. Recently, he acquired three more houses in Kamogawa, near his initial vacation rental. He's planning to repeat the success of his first oceanfront property with these new additions. Ken's approach is to find places that are unique and in a great location that can also accommodate larger groups—usually at least ten people.

Because the properties Ken owns are near the ocean people often ask him about the threat of tsunamis, earthquakes, and typhoons. He always makes sure the house is equipped with the necessary safety measures and there is an evacuation plan in place. There was a landslide nearby a few years ago, but he stays optimistic and ensures he has both earthquake and fire insurance to cover the rebuilding cost in the event of a disaster.

Ken's advice to successfully implement his strategy is to find someone you can trust who has experience in real estate, and then spend time looking at properties every day. This allows you to gain experience so when you see something you know is good, you can confidently purchase that first property.

STRATEGY: LONG-TERM MANSHON RENTAL

How it works: find and buy an old condo in a central location, renovate it, and rent it to a long-term tenant without excessive fees.

Based on advice from Canadian Senpai, this was the strategy I employed with my first renovation property—the Tree House. Canadian Senpai, who owns numerous old apartments in central locations all around Tokyo, uses this same strategy. He rents primarily to expats who appreciate his rustic style incorporating reclaimed wood and found objects. *(I share more about him, his story and his strategies in Chapter 6, "Hunting for a House.")* He also likes the idea that sometimes, when these buildings are eventually torn down, there is a chance of hitting the jackpot. Larger developers might offer you a lucrative buyout or even grant a penthouse in a high-rise if you are fortunate.

Buying affordable properties in excellent central locations, renovating them, and renting them out at fair market prices—without unnecessary fees—has become my expertise and passion in the Japanese real estate market. I have a keen eye for identifying unique and charming properties with great potential for renovation, creating appealing living spaces that set themselves apart in the market.

Instead of charging key money, gratitude money, and all of the other fees, I just bake my extra expenses into the rent. My rents are about 10–20% higher than similar apartments in the area, but overall it's a lower cost for the tenant than the traditional system. It's a huge opportunity for people with properties and a desire to rent them long-term. Just raise your rent a little bit and don't make it hard for the renter. There's a huge market for people renting in this new way in Tokyo.

My renovation approach involves preserving the original character of these properties while incorporating modern amenities, attracting tenants seeking extraordinary experiences. This not only allows for higher rental prices but also opens up opportunities to cater to niche markets, including expats and tourists, driving higher demand and occupancy rates.

Investing in distinctive and unique properties in prime locations has proven to be a rewarding and fulfilling venture. Achieving returns on my investments ranging from 5% to 15% has further solidified my belief in the immense potential of this approach. In addition, my houses have been chosen for various photoshoots by Japanese fashion magazines and TV stations. It's a source of pride to witness something I've crafted contributing to the aesthetic appeal of their pages and media projects.

STRATEGY: APARTMENT CONVERSION

> **How it works:** find and buy an abandoned home, and convert it into two living spaces—live in one and rent the other long term.

I purchased another house in Tokyo in 2020 and, lacking an inventive name, I christened it Liton House. This nearly-century-old gem occupies less than 70 m² (750 ft²) in my neighborhood. As part of my renovation of the previously abandoned home, I converted 20% of the space of this house into a studio apartment complete with its own kitchen, bathroom and shower. Now, similar to a duplex in the US, I have a place to live and my tenants' rent covers the mortgage.

One of my most cherished DIY projects in this house was crafting the kitchens. I dedicated an old Japanese oshiire (押し入れ)—a closet or storage area—to house the second kitchen. But that wasn't the only unique touch. As a nod to the house's history, I repurposed the old tokonoma (床の間)—a sacred space—and fashioned a closet within it. The house's original rounded pillar, a time-worn testament to its character, remains prominently visible. I did this all on a small budget, and I paid with my creativity and hundreds of hours in time.

The strategy of allowing your tenants to contribute to your mortgage, thereby reducing your monthly expenses, is common worldwide and not unique to Japan. But many Japanese families use this method of apartment conversion to create a generational home when constructing a new house, so multiple generations of a family can live in the same building. Given the universality of this method, I won't extensively delve into it in this book. However, I wanted to share that I've successfully implemented it here in Japan, and you can too.

STRATEGY: INVESTMENT PROPERTY CREATION

> **How it works:** find and buy an abandoned home, renovate it, rent it to a tenant then sell about a year later as an investment property.

I personally have a passion for investing in akiyas and take a hands-on approach in carefully selecting unique properties for my portfolio, such as my Sangenjaya House. I invest substantial amounts of time into designing and transforming these properties into distinctive and special spaces. On the other hand, Satoru Isono, real estate agent and the CEO of Sodateru Toushi, adopts a different approach. He operates on a larger scale, hiring companies to renovate multiple properties then making them available for rent at a more affordable price. Despite our different strategies, our ultimate goal remains the same: to breathe new life into abandoned houses and offer affordable housing solutions to various demographics.

I was introduced to Isono-san by my friend Isozaki-san as we have a lot of things in common. Before delving into the real estate industry, Isono-san worked for fifteen years as a financial advisor. The knowledge he acquired during those years has since proven advantageous in his current business within investments into abandoned Japanese houses.

Isono-san Akiya Investments
Purchase Costs

Address	Selling Price	Bought For	Reno Cost	Closing Cost
Chiba #1	3,300,000	1,643,019	524,720	167,200
Chiba #2	4,500,000	2,249,227	567,908	214,500
Chiba #3	4,800,000	2,439,059	1,135,684	224,400
Chiba #4	6,500,000	2,446,334	1,382,422	0
Niigata	1,700,000	1,206,281	579,700	198,000
Chiba #5	5,300,000	1,977,249	1,144,054	0
Chiba #6	3,500,000	1,389,221	1,373,300	0
Chiba #7	5,500,000	2,217,272	1,546,142	220,000
Chiba #8	4,700,000	1,604,903	992,004	0
Osaka	5,100,000	2,578,169	844,204	0
Chiba #9	15,500,000	11,800,000	0	560,000

Prices in Japanese Yen (¥)

Isono-san's approach is to purchase vacant properties, renovate them, find tenants and eventually sell them as investment real estate. This strategy is met with enthusiasm from local residents near these neglected properties as the renovation contributes to enhancing the community. Those living nearby the abandoned properties often face more challenges than the distant property owners themselves. Neglected vacant houses can lead to overgrown vegetation, pest infestations, and unwelcome residents like raccoons, mice, and snakes. Instances of unauthorized occupants can also raise safety concerns among the local community. Revitalizing a vacant property is typically appreciated first by the neighbors. Just recently, while cleaning up a vacant property, a neighbor kindly offered Isono-san snacks and juice, while saying, "Keep up the good work, young man!"

Isono-san Akiya Investments
Profitability

Address	Date Bought	Date Sold	Profit	% Profit	Rent / Month
Chiba #1	6.3.2020	31.10.2020	965,061	29.2	45,000
Chiba #2	21.3.2021	5.8.2021	1,468,365	32.6	60,000
Chiba #3	8.10.2019	28.12.2021	1,000,857	20.9	60,000
Chiba #4	26.4.2021	25.10.2022	2,671,244	41.1	75,000
Niigata	23.10.2020	31.10.2022	-283,981	-16.7	30,000
Chiba #5	8.3.2019	16.12.2022	2,178,697	41.1	60,000
Chiba #6	12.9.2022	31.1.2023	737,479	21.1	45,000
Chiba #7	30.7.2022	24.2.2023	1,516,586	27.6	60,000
Chiba #8	23.1.2023	12.5.2023	2,103,093	44.7	55,000
Osaka	30.11.2022	20.5.2023	1,677,627	32.9	58,000
Chiba #9	30.9.2021	28.6.2023	3,140,000	20.3	166,000

Prices in Japanese Yen (¥)

This investment strategy also provides employment opportunities for local renovation companies, presents spacious and budget-friendly detached homes for families who previously resided in cramped apartments, and is well-regarded as a high-yield, attractive investment by fellow investors. Isono-san's business provides him with a sense of fulfillment as it brings joy to the many people he encounters. He's able to rent out the houses long-term, and they all generate a return-on-investment (ROI) of 20–45%.

In addition, by choosing to be a fair and transparent landlord, Isono-san can not only provide a more equitable living arrangement for tenants but also foster long-lasting and positive rental relationships. His tenant-friendly policy of no extra fees has yielded incredible results: not one tenant has ever left his properties due to additional charges.

However, there are certain challenges to navigate. The growing attention to vacant properties in Japan has led to an uptick in property prices. Novice investors may overpay, requiring extra diligence to secure cost-effective purchases. Furthermore, instances of investors divesting properties due to unsuccessful revitalization attempts have become more common. Isono-san advises that it's crucial to exercise caution and avoid hastily acquiring properties in poor initial conditions.

Japan faces the dual challenge of increasing vacant homes due to a declining population, coupled with the problem of people struggling to find suitable, and affordable, rental housing. Landlords often discriminate against single mothers, the elderly, foreign residents, individuals with disabilities, and even pet owners. These underserved groups have a tough time finding homes that meet their needs. Isono-san has been able to provide spacious, affordable, and well-maintained detached houses to people who previously had to settle for cramped apartments. This has genuinely pleased these individuals by addressing their housing needs and enhancing their quality of life.

By renovating and renting out these abandoned properties, investors like Isono-san are not only benefiting financially but also contributing to address the housing challenges faced by foreigners and marginalized communities. This investment approach holds the promise of a socially responsible way to revitalize unused properties and address housing inequalities in Tokyo and beyond.

STRATEGY: AFFORDABLE LONG-TERM RENTALS

> **How it works:** find and buy an abandoned home, renovate it, and rent it to a long-term tenant without excessive fees.

When it comes to affordable real estate investments, my friend Ito Takashi has achieved remarkable success. Ito-san's ventures and properties have made frequent appearances on my social media platforms, drawing in a wealth of comments, impressions, and likes. Because Ito-san and Isono-san have such similar strategies, at first, I didn't plan to interview Ito-san for this book. But something changed when I saw how many questions people had for him after I posted a YouTube video online. Ito-san's strong work ethic, willingness to get his hands dirty, and impressive negotiation skills are truly impressive.[*]

---

[*] URLs for YouTube videos featuring Ito-san and one of his homes are listed in Chapter 19, "More Information."

With a background in carpentry, Ito-san possesses a keen eye for spotting cost-effective housing opportunities that require minimal maintenance. These houses may appear rundown at first glance, but with a touch of renovation magic—a fresh coat of paint, some new flooring—they're ready to be transformed into profitable rentals. Ito-san's approach is very similar to Isono-san's approach with two key differences: Ito-san does all the renovation work himself, and he generally doesn't sell the houses once he's started renting them out.

Ito-san's approach is simple. He buys the cheapest houses available, fixes them up inexpensively, and then rents them out affordably. Being a carpenter, he can ensure his tenants are happy with the maintenance. He started on this renovation journey four years ago and just acquired his eighth house. The houses he purchases have ranged anywhere from ¥435,000 (~$3,000) up to around ¥1.45 million (~$10,000), and he recently purchased a house for ¥1.16 million ($8,000). The reason many of the properties have been cheap is that either you can't rebuild them, it's crammed full of stuff, or the owner simply wants a quick cash deal.

Ito-san primarily finds these houses through two main channels: online listings and the local community. Interestingly, the house he recently purchased was sourced through a broker that he's worked with for some time. Brokers often contact him before these properties even hit the market, as they trust that he's not overly picky when it comes to the condition of the property, he pays in cash, and he's easy to work with.

After finishing the renovation, Ito-san's approach is to rent them out to tenants who may find it challenging to secure conventional rental contracts, such as single mothers and foreigners. Down the road, he might consider selling some of the houses he's renovated. Selling a house with a tenant inside is referred to as "owner

♟

Both Ito-san and Isono-san provide consulting on their business strategy. They've partnered to create a course that teaches people how to navigate the market with old houses, turning them into affordable housing for marginalized people in Japan while still making good money. The course is in Japanese, but I'm working with them to have it translated into English. To get notified when it's available, get on my mailing list on my website, the link is in the "More Information" chapter.

change" (オーナーチェンジ) in Japan, and it's an attractive option for investors, as they typically look at returns of around 10–15%. Ito-san's properties usually generate approximately 50% gross profit annually when they're rented out, which means that many of his houses could potentially sell for up to four times the price he originally paid for them.

Some of Ito-san's properties are quite far apart, so owning a car is essential for his work. For his latest venture, the akiya property he acquired in Chiba for just ¥1.16 million ($8,000), I'm considering creating a documentary-style YouTube series. The idea is to delve deep into this journey by interviewing neighbors, brokers, previous owners, and renovators, addressing various akiya-related questions. Documenting the process from abandoned, neglected, and despised by neighbors to something truly remarkable will be fascinating.

Plus, we want to capture the heartwarming moment when a big, happy family moves into Ito-san's revitalized property.

Ito-san believes the key to his success lies in knowing which properties to invest in. Additionally, having DIY and renovation skills has created a sense of security for his tenants. They trust that they won't be overcharged for minor repairs like a small hole in the wall. In fact, in the four years he's been renovating and renting, not a single tenant has moved out, which speaks volumes about the trust he's built with his tenants.

STRATEGY: NEW BUILD INVESTMENT

How it works: invest in building a brand-new house.

This book mainly focuses on the real estate market of old, abandoned houses in and around Tokyo. But I also want to highlight that there are investment opportunities outside of Tokyo, including newer properties. These types of investments are often considered safer and are more likely to receive bank loans.

By now, you may have noticed that in Japan, the predominant trend is for people to purchase new houses. Japanese individuals have a preference for new items, and banks also lean towards newer properties, simplifying the loan approval process. The gross yield from newer apartments in Tokyo, typically around 5%, is generally lower in comparison to older properties. However, if the bank assists with a cost-effective loan, it can still lead to a remarkable opportunity. While my expertise lies mainly within Tokyo's older house market, I'm thrilled to tell you about Ziv Nakajima-Magen, an experienced real estate investor from Israel with over ten years of experience in

Japan's real estate market. Ziv has extensive knowledge about invest-ing in various regions of Japan, covering both older houses and new developments. Ziv is also an accomplished author, having penned several books about real estate in Japan. His insights can provide valuable guidance for both seasoned investors and newcomers seek-ing to understand the nuances of the Japanese property market.

Ziv started his investing in the Japanese real estate market in 2011, and he's been living in Fukuoka, located in the southern part of Japan, since 2013. His investment strategy has been focusing on cash flow through residential and commercial rental properties. Around 80% of his investments are safe and stable, centered in larger metropolitan areas, family-sized properties in newer buildings with moderate yields. The remaining 20% is allocated to more adventur-ous buildings with higher-yield profiles.

Ziv has found investing in Japanese real estate enjoyable and has seen minimal surprises during the purchase, sale, and management of the properties he's owned. He's also found that for some people it can be frustrating to adapt to the pace and order of things in Japan, particularly if you're someone like Ziv who is always on the move and looking for the next opportunity.

STRATEGY: RETREAT CENTER

How it works: find an abandoned house, renovate it and turn it into a charming retreat center or getaway experience.

This isn't a strategy that I have any experience with, but I was in-trigued when I saw it being done by the renown Japanese homeware

brand Muji (無印良品). They just opened up their first retreat center, called a Muji Base, in Chiba (千葉県), where they converted
an akiya that was over a hundred years old. Situated in Kamogawa
(鴨川市), two hours outside of Tokyo, this century-old countryside home, formerly the Noda Printmaking Workshop, radiates traditional charm. Guests can book stays for two nights or more, with a
cost of ¥55,000 ($379) for three days and two nights. During their
visit, they can enjoy Muji's carefully curated packaged meals or opt
for locally sourced dishes made with seasonal ingredients. Muji goes
the extra mile with cozy pajamas, luxurious bedding, and essential
toothbrushes for a restful night's sleep. Guests can also partake in
local experiences like melon harvesting, dairy farming, and hiking.

In a forward-thinking move, Muji plans to create more Muji Bas-
es by repurposing vacant and abandoned houses throughout Japan.
These thoughtfully curated retreats provide an authentic experience
while rejuvenating the countryside, showcasing the tranquility and
beauty of rural Japan.

I believe this is a brilliant marketing strategy, and Muji beautifully demonstrates the incredible potential of akiyas. They've taken
a century-old house with a rich history in rural Japan and turned it
into a place of pure enjoyment and inspiration. This is such an unusual approach for a Japanese market and a bold move for a Japanese
company—I think it bodes well for the potential future of renovation here in Japan.

Meanwhile, as a Swede, I am just waiting for one of Muji's biggest competitors, IKEA, to enter the akiya real estate scene. IKEA is
working with similar projects in Sweden, providing affordable housing. *(URL's for Muji, the Muji Base and IKEA are all in the "More
Information" chapter at the end of this book.)*

STRATEGY: TOTAL HOME REPLACEMENT

> **How it works:** find an abandoned house in a "no-rebuild" area, take it apart by hand, leaving one pillar, then rebuild and replace the last pillar.

On the opposite end of the spectrum, I have seen companies purchase neglected houses, leave just one pillar standing, construct an entirely new structure, and then replace the pillar. Legally, it remains an old house, but in reality, it's a new one. I have no personal experience with this strategy, but have seen companies take this approach in my neighborhood. It's a clever approach to build an essentially brand-new home in an otherwise "no-rebuild" area and appeal to a traditional Japanese buyer who is looking for New.

Because, like my Sangenjaya House, these houses are built in neighborhoods with very narrow roadways, they can't just demo the house in the usual way, even if they were allowed to rebuild on the empty land (they're not). Instead they must take the entire house apart by hand then rebuild an entirely new house, by hand, in its place, all while leaving the single pillar intact so that the house is technically still the same. Everything must be carried in and out by hand and it's much more time consuming and expensive.

On the upside, the sales price is much higher than a renovated home in the same area. This is the closest thing to an American-style "house flipping" strategy as there exists in Japan, with its unique market and preferences for New. This is being done by smaller real estate companies and smaller renovation companies, and it's a very clever way to use their skills. They target akiya that are nearly ready to be torn down anyway. Once a home gets to a level of disrepair that it is a hazard—falling down—the municipality will step in and tear the house down. Once that's done there is no way to rebuild on that land, no matter what. So these companies find houses that are on the brink and buy them from the owners at exceptionally low prices.

The resulting homes are, while still technically old, completely new. Not only does that appeal to a traditional Japanese buyer, but also that buyer can get a mortgage. Usually mortgages are not available for these non-rebuildable areas of Tokyo. But the companies doing this work have relationships with the banks—the banks know the work has been done well and will make exceptions for their buyers. These homes will still not sell for as much as a brand-new, conventionally built home, but they do sell for considerably more than a renovated home in the same area.

In general, flipping is not the real opportunity here in Japan, especially for a single DIY renovator. The best opportunity is to buy cheap, renovate and turn your property into an investment property of some sort. Hold it long-term and enjoy the income. Selling those income properties later is primarily a way to free up cash for new projects, not a main source of income. But, for the right person who has a team of skilled contractors, real estate brokers, equipment, expertise and connections who wants to sell to a traditional Japanese buyer, this seems (at least from afar) to be a viable strategy.

STRATEGY: APAATO BUILDING CREATIVE SPACE

How it works: find a neglected apaato building and renovate it into a creative, collaborative space.

While I have experience in buying manshons (マンション) and free-standing houses in Tokyo, I am yet to explore the world of apaatos. I've visited friends living in these two-story houses with tiny apartments, typically around 12–20 m^2 (129–215 ft^2) akin to student housing in European cities. While I haven't lived in one, the idea of acquiring an old, not-too-run-down apaato building and transforming it into a unique collaborative space excites me. I envision working with artists, architects, and friends to decorate and design each room, creating the coolest apaato building in all of Japan, perhaps even a remarkable Airbnb.

Currently, my real estate ventures and renovation projects in Japan focus on old free-standing houses. While they require more effort and maintenance, owning the land grants me greater freedom. I can run my Airbnb business and connect with my Japanese neighbors in a different way. As I ponder future real estate ventures, I'm leaning towards free-standing houses or apaato buildings, where I solely own the land they stand on.

While Japan's population is decreasing and the amount of vacant properties are growing, the thought of people abandoning their manshons and ceasing to pay management fees worries me. Turns out that people neglect or abandon apartments just as they do free-standing houses, and when they do, they usually stop paying the maintenance fees and the building gets run down. By owning a building entirely, I could take responsibility for its upkeep and renovations. As someone without a 9–5 job, I have the flexibility to manage renovations and ensure the property stays in top shape. And I love doing it too.

Ultimately, the choice between living in a manshon or an apaato, or opting for a free-standing house, depends on individual preferences and needs. We are all unique, and our housing choices reflect our lifestyles and desires. While I may have a crazy dream of creating the coolest apaato building in Japan, I'm open to embracing new opportunities and discovering what the future holds in the world of Japanese real estate.

MY FINAL THOUGHTS ON INVESTMENT STRATEGIES

While there are many different successful investment strategies you can make in the Japanese market, and I have my personal preferences, there's one that I would not recommend in the Japanese market: flipping—buying a run-down house with the goal of fixing it up quickly and selling it at a profit. A common real-estate strategy in the US, by now I hope you understand why that strategy won't work here in Japan. Even if you don't plan to keep the properties as long-term rentals, you will still need to rent them for a year or two to prove they generate income. Then you can sell them as an investment property.

Whichever strategy you choose, I wish you the best of luck! It may be my European bias showing, but I want to see more people saving these beautiful old homes and creating something special. If Sangenjaya House had been on a regular road with a re-buildable lot just a few blocks away, it would have been sold just for the land it was standing on at ¥1.5 million per square meter ($961 per square foot). The new owner or developer would have taken two days to tear the house down, then a week later a new concrete foundation would have been on the ground. Next, a brand-new three-story house. *New*, but, in my humble opinion, lacking character or soul.

There's so many other ways to approach older homes. I hope you try one.

🔑 5

Understanding Akiya

kiya toushi (空き家投資), the art of investing in abandoned houses, presents an enticing opportunity for those seeking to enter the world of real estate in Japan. This simple concept involves acquiring neglected properties at bargain prices, renovating them cost-effectively, and offering them as affordable rentals. I personally have embraced this investment strategy and have purchased several akiyas for my own portfolio, including my Sangenjaya House.

The number of abandoned houses in Japan continues to rise creating lucrative financial prospects and also creates opportunities to revitalize abandoned spaces and provide more affordable housing options for people. With low acquisition costs and the potential for high returns, more and more people are exploring akiya toushi as a solid investment strategy.

As I explained earlier, I started my real estate journey in Japan by buying my Tree House close to Shibuya. This cute little 39 m^2 (420 ft^2) manshon is on the top two floors of a four-story building, and

I renovated it in my iconic Scandinavian style. I didn't use expensive materials, but with great sunlight and a touch of nature the renovation looks amazing. I then moved on to buying bigger akiyas, also in central Tokyo. My Sangenjaya House is one of these properties. My free standing houses have one thing in common—except of course that they were all akiya—and that is that they are located on small, picturesque streets that are non-rebuildable.

Sai kenchi fukanō (再建築不可能) in Japanese.

Land such as residential land must be adjacent to roads that can be safely used as emergency vehicles and evacuation routes according to regulations. This is because if the property is only adjacent to narrow passages, fire engines and ambulances cannot pass through in the event of a disaster, and there is a risk that it will lead to further damage.

In the world of abandoned houses in Japan, I've found that this fascinating niche often goes unnoticed—properties situated on roads less than two meters wide (6.5 feet). While you may not be allowed to rebuild these houses, I saw a unique opportunity to renovate them. These properties may not be popular among Japanese buyers who prefer new constructions, but I believe they hold immense potential.

In my area, these abandoned houses are priced at just a quarter of the value of land adjacent to wider roads. So this became my niche—a hidden treasure waiting to be discovered—and now the secret is out. The location is excellent, and the community is strong, providing a perfect foundation for a successful venture. With a lower buy-in point and steady rental income, the yield is remarkably high.

There's also an exciting possibility for future gains. If the government decides to widen the road, the land's value could skyrocket fourfold or even more. It's like holding a potential lottery ticket, with the chance of a significant windfall in the market. While the timing is uncertain—it could be 5 years, 50 years, or never—the potential rewards make it a venture worth considering.

It's mind-boggling, isn't it? Right in the heart of the city, you have these amazing houses with a staggering 75% discount, just because of the narrow road in front of them. And no one seems to be interested in these properties! It's like everyone else is blind to this incredible opportunity, leaving these prime properties untouched and abandoned. Well, everyone except for me and some savvy Japa-

🔑

Renting out these properties long-term offers an impressive return-on-investment (ROI) of around 10-15%, while using Airbnb can yield an astounding 100% ROI.

However, these calculations do not account for the countless hours and effort I pour into renovating these houses, turning them into unique and vibrant spaces. You can witness the entire renovation process on my YouTube series, *Tokyo Renovation Diaries*, giving you a visual glimpse into the challenges of buying and renovating a house in Japan.

nese real estate investment companies who see the potential lottery ticket. These companies are snatching up these properties, keeping them empty and abandoned, just waiting for that possible lottery win when the government decides to widen the road.

The catch is, despite the amazing discount on purchasing these properties, you can't get one of the favorable housing loans. Instead, you have to opt for an investment loan with a higher interest rate.

HOW DO THESE HOUSES AFFECT THE NEIGHBORHOOD?

In Japan, it can be challenging to dispose of trash, and some abandoned houses become makeshift junkyards, causing distress to nearby residents. In cases where there is a direct threat of fires or imminent structural collapse, the local municipality may intervene and tear down the house.

I have personally witnessed several instances in my area where the local municipality has taken action. They have built walls* around abandoned houses or collectively decided to tear them down to maintain the aesthetics and safety of the neighborhood. This sense of communal responsibility and pride in preserving their surroundings showcases the municipality's proactive approach to addressing abandoned properties.

For example, in my area the municipality was getting a lot of complaints about a house that was only about 100 m (328 ft) from my own. It was an eighty-year-old house that no one had lived in for over twenty years. Everyone in the neighborhood knew it was an abandoned house, so people started dumping their trash—things they usually had to pay for to get rid of like mattresses, old vacu-

---

* There is a video on my channel of what these walls look like. The URL is in the "More Information" chapter near the end of this book.

um cleaners and sofas. There were microwaves piled up from the 1980s. The Japanese call this a gomi yashiki (ゴミ屋敷), a "garbage mansion." All this trash filled the whole house, and while it wasn't smelly, the view was crazy with things stacked on top of each other all around the house. The walls were falling apart. The house was ready to be torn down. The people who were living close by were very unhappy.

Then one day everything was just gone, and all that was left was a plot of empty land. It seemed like the house had just mysteriously vanished in the night—the municipality had taken it all away.

Termite damage is a big contributing factor to the deterioration of these homes, but the humid climate doesn't help either. The summer here can be quite warm, often 40 °C (104 °F) with humidity of 70–80%—very warm, raining, and wet. Summer is the rainy season and it rains every day. It will often rain for fifteen minutes, then be sunny the rest of the day. Japanese people use umbrellas because it's so humid that if something gets wet it will never dry out. If you aren't using an umbrella when it's raining people will look at you funny and think you are very poor. Same with the house—if you have a water leak then it gets in and never dries out. So it rots. Then August is hot and it turns into a sauna. The winter in Tokyo is gray. Tokyo is about ten degrees warmer than where I lived in Sweden, and it snows about one day per year here in Tokyo. While the temperature can drop below freezing it doesn't happen long enough or often enough in order to kill the termites and other pests. Those pests then can spread to the nearby homes.

Between the weather and the termites, even a beautifully built house will eventually collapse if it isn't maintained. If you live in the US or Europe, you already know that a well-maintained house can stand for a hundred years or more, but a poorly maintained one will disintegrate within a decade or two. Because Japanese homes depreciate to a value of zero in twenty-two years, there's no incentive to maintain them, though they do keep them very clean. If they are abandoned, they fall apart very, very quickly.

Three weeks ago there was a story on the news about an abandoned house that collapsed. It's a real hazard and a big reason why both neighbors and the municipality want to see these houses taken care of.

WHY ARE THESE HOUSES ABANDONED?

Setagaya (世田谷区), often called the "Brooklyn of Tokyo," is Tokyo's largest ward both in terms of size and population. It's known for popular neighborhoods like Futago Tamagawa, Shimokitazawa, and Sangenjaya. Japan's overall population is decreasing, but Setagaya's population keeps growing and will likely continue until the 2050s. Despite this growth, there are over 50,000 abandoned houses in Setagaya, with a population of around 1 million people. There are more abandoned houses in Setagaya than any other ward in Tokyo. To give you some perspective, during my time in New York, I hardly ever saw a single abandoned house.

When the municipality asked akiya owners in Setagaya: "What issues do you face when trying to make use of your Akiya?"* their answers fell into these categories:

- **Not enough time:** owners are too busy with work to deal with their akiya

---

* Source: Setagaya Ward Vacant House Countermeasures Plan, 2018 "世田谷区空家等対策計画"

- **Age and health:** owners are getting older or facing health issues, making it difficult to do anything with their akiya
- **Money problems:** owners want to fix up their akiya, but they don't have the funds to do so
- **Demolition dilemma:** owners want to tear down their property, but they can't afford to do so
- **Paperwork and bureaucracy:** owners don't know how to deal with the paperwork or red tape of inheriting their akiya

There are numerous reasons why houses become abandoned and left vacant. Japanese people often have a different perspective on houses compared to Europeans and Americans. While land is considered valuable and appreciates over time, in Japan the value of an old house depreciates. As a result, when someone passes away, their property might be sold cheaply, but more often than not, they are simply left unused due to their age and perceived lack of value by the owner or inheritor.

Research from 2020 revealed significant insights into the issue of vacant houses in Japan. The study surveyed 300 individuals in their 30s to 60s who owned vacant properties in Tokyo, Chiba, Saitama, and Kanagawa prefectures.

Here are some key findings from the study:

- Nearly half of the owners of detached houses and condominiums had left their properties vacant for over five years, leading to a social problem of neglected and unattended houses.
- Negative perceptions related to "money" were prevalent among respondents. Top concerns included the inability to sell the property (32.4%), renovation costs (23.6%), and high property tax (25.6%).

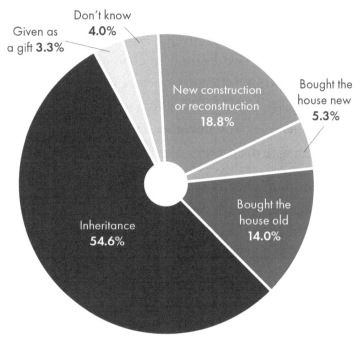

How did you acquire your akiya?

- As age increased, the perception of not being able to sell or renovate the house also grew. The older generation was more aware of the challenges and expenses associated with vacant properties.
- Despite the challenges, over 70% of respondents expressed interest in utilizing their vacant houses, with 85.2% of detached house owners and 64.8% of condominium owners having left their properties unoccupied for at least a year.

The research highlights the complexities surrounding vacant houses in Japan and the strong desire among owners to utilize these properties. It also sheds light on the financial and logistical challenges that often deter owners from making use of their vacant houses.

How far away do you live from your akiya?

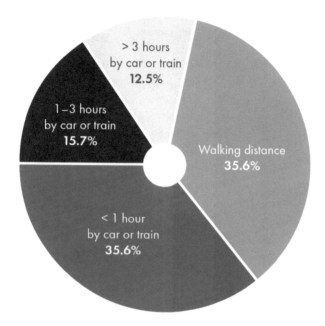

> 3 hours
by car or train
12.5%

1–3 hours
by car or train
15.7%

Walking distance
35.6%

< 1 hour
by car or train
35.6%

Imagine yourself in the shoes of the owner of these abandoned houses—they hold sentimental value and memories, making it difficult to part with the property. However, if you can locate the owner and show genuine interest in their property, promising to revitalize it with love and care, they might be more inclined to let go of an unused property that they continue to pay taxes on.

WHY DON'T THE OWNERS TEAR THEIR ABANDONED HOUSES DOWN?

The easy explanation for why owners of abandoned houses in Japan don't tear them down boils down to one thing—financial considerations.

What are the reasons for keeping your akiya?

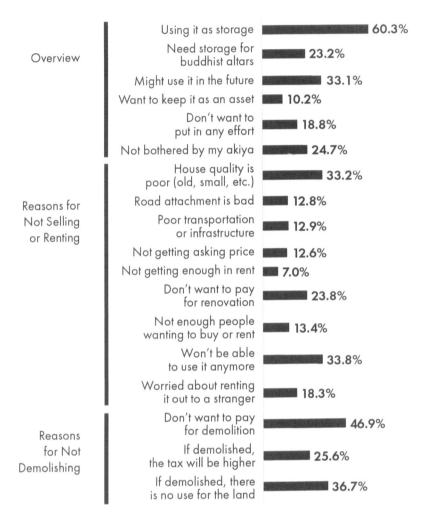

Overview	Using it as storage	60.3%
	Need storage for buddhist altars	23.2%
	Might use it in the future	33.1%
	Want to keep it as an asset	10.2%
	Don't want to put in any effort	18.8%
	Not bothered by my akiya	24.7%
Reasons for Not Selling or Renting	House quality is poor (old, small, etc.)	33.2%
	Road attachment is bad	12.8%
	Poor transportation or infrastructure	12.9%
	Not getting asking price	12.6%
	Not getting enough in rent	7.0%
	Don't want to pay for renovation	23.8%
	Not enough people wanting to buy or rent	13.4%
	Won't be able to use it anymore	33.8%
	Worried about renting it out to a stranger	18.3%
Reasons for Not Demolishing	Don't want to pay for demolition	46.9%
	If demolished, the tax will be higher	25.6%
	If demolished, there is no use for the land	36.7%

In contrast to countries like Sweden or the United States, where "in need of renovation" properties are sought after for their potential, the perception of old houses in Japan is quite different. In the Japanese real estate market, "old" is often associated with "bad," making it challenging to sell or rent out such properties.

Demolishing an old house in Japan can be costly due to trash disposal costs and the cost of demolition, dissuading owners from taking that route. As a result, they might choose to leave the property as is to avoid the financial burden. In addition, land without structures on it is subject to much higher property taxes. Therefore, it's cheaper to keep the abandoned house on the property than to face increased property tax rates.

For those with financial resources and time, renovating, selling, or demolishing the property might be viable options. However, not everyone can afford these solutions, leading them to leave the property as is. It's essential to understand that in Japan most abandoned houses are not available for sale on traditional online platforms. This is where working with a local broker becomes invaluable. A knowledgeable broker can identify potential sellers who may be willing to part with their abandoned properties, relieving them of the burden while presenting you with the renovation opportunity.

WHAT IF YOU CAN'T FIND THE OWNER?

In the bustling city of Shibuya, there are countless abandoned houses with owners seemingly impossible to locate. Despite the land being worth a fortune, hundreds of Japanese real estate companies have attempted to find the owners, but to no avail. As long as these properties do not pose a direct danger to their surroundings, the municipality typically takes no action.

If you find yourself unable to locate the owner of an abandoned house, leaving a small note in the post box might be a considerate gesture, but it's essential to move on and explore other options. Sometimes your local broker may be able to help in these cases. I've found success by asking neighbors of the abandoned properties. Of-

THE RADIATION MYTH

One common misconception that frequently surfaces on my social media is the belief that "all these houses are abandoned because of radiation." It is essential to clarify this myth and provide a more accurate picture of the situation.

Indeed, after the great earthquake that struck Japan in 2011, the Fukushima region experienced severe repercussions, leading to the abandonment of some houses due to radiation concerns. During my visit to Minami Soma, which was significantly affected during that time, I witnessed firsthand the impact on certain villages that were completely abandoned overnight.

It is crucial to emphasize that this scenario is not representative of Japan as a whole. While there have been instances of houses being abandoned due to radiation concerns, you should understand that this is a localized issue rather than a widespread phenomenon across the entire country.

In reality, the majority of abandoned houses in Japan are not related to radiation but are a result of various other factors, such as aging populations, changing demographics, economic shifts, and urban migration. Many older properties have been left unattended due to changing lifestyles and preferences for newer and more convenient living arrangements.

ten a property is abandoned but the owners check in on the property infrequently and one of the neighbors may know how to contact them. Making friends with the neighbors is always helpful in these cases.

BE THE NEIGHBOR EVERYONE LOVES

Abandoned houses can be a thorn in the side for neighbors, posing risks like fires, earthquakes, termites, and unruly gardens. But imagine being the one to transform that eyesore into a charming abode. When you buy an abandoned house and breathe new life into it, you're not just investing in property—you're investing in your community.

Your efforts don't go unnoticed. Neighbors will appreciate your commitment to revitalizing the neighborhood. You're not only enhancing the aesthetics but also creating a safer and more vibrant environment. Your neighbors will love the positive change you bring, and your actions could inspire others to follow suit.

In my experience, my neighbors came to praise me repeatedly for taking on my renovation projects. These interactions underscore the importance of becoming an integral part of the community (if you can) before making a property purchase. When you actively contribute and integrate yourself into the neighborhood, people are more likely to share hidden gems with you—houses that may not even be on the market. These are homes that owners and neighbors are concerned about, properties they want someone to rescue, nurture, and care for with genuine affection.

The other week one of my neighbors approached me with an old rundown house in my area that they politely asked me to buy or revitalize on a rental contract. Maybe this will be my next renovation project, only time will tell.

Thinking back to my own childhood in Älvsjö, just south of Stockholm, I remember how well I knew the streets. I biked with my friends, explored BMX tracks, and had our first taste of freedom at Lake Långsjön. It's remarkable that I can count the abandoned houses on just one hand—only three in my neighborhood.

Close to my middle school, Johan Skytte Skolan, was an old abandoned mental hospital known as "Långbro Asylum." It was famous internationally. Even the German Nazi Hermann Göring was rumored to have been treated there. This place was perfect for a horror movie, and it was said that Sweden's most dangerous woman, Elisabet, still lurked there, even though the hospital had closed. The place was a sprawling park with a big pond similar in size to Central Park in New York.

The hospital closed in 1997 and remained empty for almost ten years. As a teenager, I had the thrilling, if scary, experience of sneaking into these buildings with my friends during summer holidays. The old structures were all connected by underground tunnels, and exploring them with just a flashlight, passing small fire trucks and hospital beds, left quite an impression. I'll never forget the time when my friend John turned off the flashlight and started making spooky sounds—we all panicked and ran for the exit.

Those old Långbro Asylum buildings have now become luxury apartments. I remember there was a debate when these apartments were built. "Could you live in an old mental hospital?" But they sold out quickly, and the whole park has been turned into a lovely place with cafés, gardens, and happy families.

It's a remarkable transformation, and I can't help but wonder if an abandoned Japanese mental hospital could undergo the same transformation into luxury apartments. Maybe one day.

🔑 6

Hunting for a House

Soon after I moved to Japan, my Italian friend Timothée was looking at a place on Craigslist—an apartment in Shibuya—to rent for a few months while he came here for modeling. Timothée asked me if I could take a look at it for him. I wanted to help him out, and plus I was curious, so I went up to Shibuya to look at the apartment.

I arrived at the address to find an old, rundown building with graffiti on the facade. The elevator seemed run down as well, which seemed a little odd. On the fourth floor, I knocked on the door to the apartment and it moved—it was already open. I probably imagined the creak as it swung open a little, but either way it was creepy. I texted the owner to see what was going on, and it turned out he'd left the door open and had been waiting for me downstairs. I had just missed him on the sidewalk.

The owner came up and welcomed me into the apartment. He was a white man, mid-50s, casual clothes. He looked like any other foreign tourist in Japan. After that less-than-appealing first impression, I was unsure about what I would find, but the apartment was really cute. It was small, about 20 m² (215 ft²), with wood floors, concrete walls, and a small balcony. A charming, cozy little home.

I asked him how he had gotten ahold of the apartment, and he said that he owned it. I was still living in the share house at the time, so I was both surprised and curious.

"Foreigners can own a place in Japan?" I asked.

"Yes," he said, "you can buy houses in Chiba for cheap."

He told me if I could free up some money it would be a great investment for me to renovate one. He said I could buy a house in Chiba (千葉県)—an area just east of Tokyo—for ¥1.5–3 million ($10–20k).

I was fascinated. I told him that I really wanted to buy an apartment in Tokyo. He hesitated a moment, and then, almost like a guilty confession, he said he'd bought the apartment we were standing in about ten years earlier for about ¥7.25 million ($50,000). I asked him why the outside of the building looked so bad and he said he didn't own the building, just the apartment, so unfortunately, he had no control over it. *(Just as I mentioned in Chapter 4, "Exploring Investment Strategies," this can be a concern when you don't own the entire building.)*

I was getting excited now, thinking about the possibilities. I said that my thinking was to buy something centrally located so it would increase in value, and would be easy to rent out if I didn't end up living in Japan.

Again, he hesitated for a moment, but then he shared with me that he has many units, around fifteen or so, all in central Tokyo. He'd originally rented them all as Airbnb's, but after the Japanese

In 2018, Japan made it illegal to run an Airbnb without
a license, so it is essentially that you are properly licensed
before running an Airbnb. I cover this extensively in Chapter
14, "Operating an Airbnb," but there's a good reason why
apartments in Japan are almost never Airbnb's under these
new laws. In order to run an Airbnb in an apartment, you
have to get kyoka (許可), permission, from not only the
building manager, but also all the other apartment owners.
There is always someone who says, "no, I don't want a
hotel in my house", and it only takes one person to say no
to have your permission denied. This is why my Tree House
manshon apartment is a long-term rental. I did try for the
Airbnb license, but I couldn't get everyone in the building
to agree.

government had cracked down on Airbnb's earlier that year, he'd
converted them all to long-term rentals, renting primarily to other
expats and long-stay visitors.

We ended up talking for over two hours about the real estate
market. He told me stories about all of his apartments and showed
me pictures of all the DIY renovations he had done. Sometimes,
while we were talking, he would hesitate, almost as if considering
whether he was sharing too much. No one in or around him or the
neighborhood knew the extent to which he had these holdings, and

he wanted to keep it that way. But I was so interested and curious, and it was the first time that someone had been genuinely interested in what he was doing and he couldn't help but want to talk about it.

We exchanged phone numbers. Every time I went through Shibuya I would stop and talk to him. He was always around fixing or renovating something—always dressed in casual clothes and looking like any normal foreigner in Tokyo. He became "Canadian Senpai" to me. In Japan, a senpai (先輩) is a person who is in a higher position than you in terms of skill, age, experience or social status, someone who can guide you. A mentor. If I didn't have shootings or castings I would go find him and we would drink coffee and walk the city, looking for abandoned houses and rundown apartment buildings—renovation opportunities.

Canadian Senpai taught me how to navigate in the big city, tips and tricks about real estate in Tokyo, and how to buy shitty vacant apartments in the city center, strip them, renovate them creatively and rent them out long term. He lived in a gigantic 150 m² (1615 ft²) penthouse apartment, right in Shibuya, overlooking the most expensive newly-built apartment buildings in central Tokyo. It had been an office space previously, but he turned it into an apartment with tiles, natural reclaimed wood—it was beautiful. Lots of south facing windows, too. A big, bright, stunning apartment.

When Canadian Senpai renovates a place he usually strips the apartment down to its studs. Often he leaves the concrete exposed, giving a loft-like, slightly industrial feel. He often uses reclaimed materials, or repurposes things he's found for free, turning his places into strikingly beautiful homes. The traditional Japanese approach would be to cover the concrete with plasterboard and wallpaper, but Canadian Senpai mostly rents his places to foreigners who appreciate his design aesthetic. Plus, he doesn't charge all the extra fees which foreigners don't understand, and don't want to pay.

HOW TO FIND A HOUSE TO INVEST IN

Having invested thousands of hours researching Tokyo's real estate market, I can confidently say that the most reliable method involves working with a traditional broker and employing traditional methods. Through my personal journey, I have found this to be the most effective way to secure cheap properties and ensure a smooth and successful transaction. As an avid real estate enthusiast, I still use the most used portals on a weekly basis—Suumo and Athome— not only for research purposes but also because it's genuinely fun to check the market! In Sweden, there's a word, hemnetknarka, for the delightful addiction of being hooked on the real estate listings and always checking to see what's there. Hemnet is a Swedish real estate listing website similar to Zillow in the US, and hemnetknarka means, roughly, "high on the drug of Hemnet."

WALK THE AREA & CONTACT A BROKER

Once you know what area you are interested in, I would recommend you walk around in the area and feel the atmosphere. Do you like the area? Why do you like the area? Could you live here? We are all different people and are looking for different things. What do you like and do you have the budget to live there? Is it an area ripe for investments? Is an Airbnb, or your preferred strategy, doable?

This is when I use Suumo's map search. It's great. There's weird listings out there, too, so contact a broker and go have a look in per-

🔑

STEP-BY-STEP GUIDE TO BUY A CHEAP HOUSE IN JAPAN

- **Choose Your Desired Area:** Pick the area in Japan where you want to live or invest. Consider things like convenience, amenities, and the vibe of the neighborhood.
- **Talk to a Broker:** Get in touch with a local real estate broker. It's better to visit their office in person to build a stronger connection.
- **Ask for Similar Listings:** Tell the broker what you're looking for in a house and ask them to show you similar properties that fit your preferences. If you don't like any of the listings the agent provided you, do your own research in the area.
- **Check Out the Houses:** Go with the broker to see the houses you liked. This will help you understand the properties better and see if they match what you need.
- **Communicate and Ask Questions:** Talk to the broker, ask questions, and get to know more about the properties. Being friendly and respectful will make them more willing to help you.
- **Be Courteous:** Show politeness and appreciation for the broker's time and effort. Respect is important in Japanese culture and will make your relationship better.

- **Do Your Research:** After the viewings, do thorough research on the properties you liked. Look into the neighborhood, transportation options, and any possible renovation costs. Ask yourself: is this house an asset or a liability?
- **Seek Expert Advice:** If you're unsure about anything, ask for advice from local experts or people who have bought houses in Japan before.
- **Make Your Decision:** Weigh the pros and cons of each property and choose the one that suits you best in terms of budget and preferences.
- **Negotiate and Finalize:** Work with the broker to negotiate the best deal for the house you want. Sort out all the legal paperwork properly.
- **Get Professional Help:** Consider hiring a legal professional to guide you through the legal processes and paperwork.
- **Celebrate Your New Home:** Once everything is settled, celebrate becoming a homeowner in Japan and make your new house your dream home.

son. Look around on Suumo and Athome* at what's available for sale, find a listing and contact the broker. The broker will guide you through the process and you can ask him any question you want to ask, as he will get a commission if the sale goes through. He most likely won't show you the cheapest properties as his commission will be lower, but you never know. Don't like your broker? Reach out to another one. Most properties don't have exclusive rights to sell to one broker. If they do have exclusive rights, however, it might be even easier to negotiate the price down since they will take a commission from both sides.

How can you identify vacant properties?

It does take a lot of footwork, but you will learn a lot and if you are lucky, you might have found yourself a new house. Take a stroll in the area where you desire to find a vacant house. Look for key indicators such as a lack of maintenance or the presence of overgrown weeds around the entrance, suggesting it might have been left unattended for an extended period. It's crucial to exercise caution, however, as some seemingly vacant houses may still have occupants. Before making any assumptions, inquire with neighbors. Talk to people. Reach out to local real estate brokers first, and if they don't handle such properties, ask people in the neighboring areas or nearby shops for any information they might have. Be honest about your intention to find a vacant house for purchase and inquire about the property's owner. Be polite, show respect, show that you want to be a part of the community.

This is exactly how I was able to buy the Sangenjaya House (more about that in the next chapter).

If you can't find any information through neighbors, you can

---

* URL's are listed in Chapter 19, "More Information."

check the register at the Legal Affairs Bureau. By visiting the bureau, called Homukyoku (法務局) in Japanese, you can obtain information about the owner of a property. Even if you aren't the owner, you can request access to the registry, which proves beneficial when trying to identify the property's current owner. Japan can be pretty analog and there is no registry online to find this information.

The Legal Affairs Bureau will provide you with vital details such as the address number and house number, aiding in your search. Keep in mind that a fee of about ¥450 (~$3) will be charged for each certificate of registered matters obtained. With these methods, you can increase your chances of finding the perfect vacant house that suits your needs and preferences.

I travel Tokyo by bicycle and am always looking for interesting architecture and renovation opportunities. I can point out all the vacant houses in my area and a dozen in the Shibuya area. This is prime real estate worth many millions of dollars. Most of these houses have been empty and abandoned for decades and these listings will most likely never reach the local, open market like most empty houses in your home market would have done.

HOW I BOUGHT THE LITON HOUSE

Just prior to the COVID epidemic, my dad came to visit me in Japan. My dad was interested in seeing some old houses just for fun. It was like when you're on vacation somewhere and you think, "Wouldn't it be great to live here?" And there's a local corner real estate office with property listings taped up in the windows, and you stand on the sidewalk and daydream about which house you want to buy. That's exactly what we did, except we went into the office to ask for some house tours as well. They greeted us with oshibori (お

しぼり) and cups of green tea. An oshibori is a hot, wet, hand towel used to clean your hands before eating. It's offered in restaurants as a common etiquette in Japan, more or less anywhere there is food—it says to you "this place is clean." We said we wanted to look at some old houses, so the broker grabbed a list of five houses and drove us around in a tiny little car to see them.

That's the day I saw the house that would later become Liton House. I was very interested in the house but wasn't really looking seriously for another project at the time. Later, at the beginning of the COVID epidemic, before everything was shut down, the broker contacted me. He said, "I'll give you the house for 30% off, and I'll get you 100% financing." I'd been turned down for financing before from the same bank the broker suggested, but because the broker had a relationship with the bank, I was approved. Not just for a mortgage, for a 100% mortgage. Incredible. The deal just fell into my lap.

NO ONE WANTS TO HELP YOU FIND A CHEAP HOUSE

Japan is a country with a myriad of middlemen, and attempting to navigate the real estate market alone can be overwhelming. This is where working with brokers can be a game-changer. Not only do they possess the expertise and market knowledge, but they also have valuable connections that can unlock off-market deals, giving you access to properties that may not be publicly listed. By collaborating with brokers, you not only save time and effort but also contribute to the local community. These professionals are well-versed in the ins and outs of the area, and supporting their services means bolstering the local economy. It's a win-win situation where you get the guidance you need, and at the same time, you actively participate in the growth and development of the Japanese communities you wish to be a part of.

Be aware that even brokers might hesitate to assist you, as their income relies on commissions. The difference in their commission for the sale of an affordable house compared to a newly-built luxury condo is significant. This can lead them to steer you towards pricier options. Also, and I can't emphasize this enough: you have to be here in Japan. If you are here then they will help you, at least somewhat, out of politeness. But no one is going to help you remotely. It's just not in their best interests to do so.

ALWAYS BE LEARNING

I am approached daily by people seeking advice and assistance. Many are drawn to the idea of acquiring a free house, but they often overlook the underlying challenges that come with it. My journey in Japan has taught me the importance of thorough research, understanding the local laws, and being aware of the potential risks and liabilities. Owning property in Japan comes with risks and responsibilities that many people don't fully understand. Even if the property is cheap or free.

I can't stress enough the significance of studying Japan, its economy, and the intricacies of its property market. Merely reading this book isn't really enough; it requires genuine dedication to understanding the nuances that intertwine and shape the real estate landscape. While I'm eager to help others and support Japan's growth, I believe that the best way to navigate this complex landscape is through knowledge and preparation.

Do your research and immerse yourself in the knowledge of Japan and its real estate market. You will have fun. Seek guidance from professionals, especially brokers who have the expertise and connections to help you navigate the process seamlessly. With a strong foundation of knowledge and the right support, you can turn your dream of owning property in Japan into a reality, setting yourself up for a rewarding and enriching experience.

Having immersed myself in the world of Japanese real estate and buying properties in Japan, I can confidently say that my knowledge far surpasses that of the average Japanese citizen. I am constantly on the lookout for new opportunities in the market, scouring listings and identifying hidden gems. In fact, I've even shared potential properties I've found with friends, some of whom have gone on to purchase those very places.

When I was hanging out with Canadian Senpai we would go to lunch and all of his real estate friends would be there. Sometimes there were big-time real estate developers there, and I was "hanging with the big boys." I didn't dare to talk to them at the time.

One of Canadian Senpai's friends, Kawamura-san, would drive from far away on his 50cc moped to meet us for lunch. Kawamura-san is a teacher by day, but he's also a licensed real estate agent who owns more than fifty real estate properties—and nobody in his life knows. He says, "Nobody knows I do real estate." But he also gets all the benefits of having a full-time job when he's applying for mortgages to buy his investment properties. It's brilliant.

Kawamura-san was the one who really encouraged me to purchase the Tree House. "Just do it!" he said.

I had the opportunity to repay the favor to Kawamura-san when I introduced him to a property in Yokohama. Like I said, I'm always scanning the market. It's fun to go virtual house hunting. What could I do with this one, how would that one work? What if I had ¥15 million (~$100,000) to spend, what could I buy? What if I had ¥1.5 billion ($10,000,000)? I even go to open houses just so I can see the insides of the properties. Yes, I'm experiencing a little hemnetknarka. (I know my house-hooked US and European friends know what I mean.)

One day when I was sifting through listings once again, I found this nice-looking house in Yokohama (横浜) with a 400 m² (4,300 ft²) garden full of charming stones and big pine trees. Having a garden that size even in that location is crazy—it's huge by Japanese standards. The place was listed for ¥10 million (~$64,000), and I thought there must be something wrong. It was way too cheap, even for an abandoned home. I showed it to Kawamura-san.

He said, "If this is the price, I'm going to buy it, are you sure you don't want it?"

I said, "I don't know anything about Yokohama. No, you go for it."

At the time, Kawamura-san was expecting his first child and was actually looking for a family home, something with a garden. I went with him to see the house and he ended up buying it, renovating it, and he lives there now with his family. Because he's a broker he was able to negotiate on the price and got the house for 25% less than the already heavily discounted list price.

OTHER STRATEGIES

Akiya Banks

Akiya banks (空き家バンク), also known as "vacant house banks" or "empty house banks," are databases that list vacant and abandoned properties. Akiya banks are not actual banks that would lend you money; they are centralized platforms or databases where municipalities can list vacant properties in their respective areas. These listings typically include details about the properties, such as location, size, condition, and price. These (data) banks were established through a government initiative to promote the utilization and revitalization of these neglected houses by connecting potential buyers with available akiya properties.

Operated by different local governments at various levels, such as city, town, village, or prefecture, each akiya bank exhibits unique characteristics. Sometimes, local real estate agencies can act as akiya banks as well. While they can vary in scale, with some featuring dozens of regularly updated listings and others having a short and rarely updated list, they share the common challenge of using a wide variety of data systems, leading to incomplete property information and subpar photos. The fees for using akiya banks generally differ, but in most cases you don't have to pay the 3% broker fee. There are two "official" nationwide akiya banks and several local ones. *(See Chapter 19, "More Information," for links to some of these.)*

Foreign media often highlights the akiya banks and encourages people to use them. In my opinion, the foreign media have this wrong. While you should be aware of akiya banks, as they are one place to look for properties, most of the akiya are not listed in the banks. When I started looking there were nearly no akiya listed in Tokyo at all, despite there being close to one million abandoned homes. I believe the methods I've shared are much more effective than spending your time searching through the akiya banks.

The situation may be different with rural Japan, and akiya banks may indeed be a good resource if you want to purchase in a rural area. I have no experience with purchasing through akiya banks, as I prefer using a local broker instead. Get to know the area and community you're interested in, and once you become a part of it, locals will likely point you to neglected properties, making akiya banks unnecessary. With over 8.5 million abandoned houses in Japan, many people know someone with, or live next to, an akiya.

In short, becoming part of the community can lead you to great opportunities. While akiya banks might be helpful, your presence and interest in revitalizing the area may open doors to unique properties not listed elsewhere.

Auction—Bank Retaken Properties

Bank retaken properties, called kyoubai bukken (競売物件) in Japanese, are a type of real estate property that becomes available when someone who borrowed money with their property as collateral can't repay the loan. In such cases, the property is taken over by the court and sold through an auction.

Auction properties can include various types of real estate, such as houses, apartments, offices, shops, and even agricultural land and forests. The key difference is that they are sold through a bidding process in the court, rather than in the regular market, using a silent bidding process.

The good thing about auction properties is that they can often be bought at less than their usual market value—even considering the low prices of abandoned homes. It's a great chance to find unique properties that are not easily available on the general market, like oddly shaped land or buildings in special areas. However, there are challenges. You may not have much information about the property as there is no broker who gets incentive or commission to help you acquire these objects. It's essential to do your own research and determine a reasonable bid amount. Investing in auction properties can be rewarding, but it requires careful consideration and understanding of the process.

One of my favorite places to explore properties online are the kyoubai (競売), auction sites in Tokyo. The listings are straightforward, without any involvement from brokers trying to make them look more appealing, and provide the raw numbers and information about the properties. Most of the properties I come across on these sites require significant restoration work, which can be both exciting and challenging.

While I've explored the auction sites, I have never bought a property at auction due to its complicated process. I've visited the court to research several properties in my area, but the experience was not as pleasant as I had hoped. In the physical courtroom, hundreds of real estate sharks from investment companies compete fiercely, and the atmosphere feels tense and secretive, with Japanese brokers screaming and fighting with each other. This is not for me.

One of the challenges of auction properties is the silent bidding process, making it difficult to estimate the final price. In central Tokyo, a highly competitive real estate market, the presence of these "sharks" in the auction room further emphasized the tough competition and the complexity of the auction process.

While auctioned properties may not be my preferred method in central Tokyo, I am open to the idea that there might be more rural areas where auctioned properties still offer a viable way to acquire houses. Each region may have its unique market dynamics, and it's essential to explore all possibilities before making investment decisions.

In the end, I enjoy the thrill of searching for hidden gems and unconventional properties, but I also value transparency and clarity in the real estate market, which is why I continue to explore various avenues to find the best investment opportunities for myself and my friends.

Acquire a Real Estate License

Another potential way to find a house is to get your own Japanese real estate license by passing the takken (宅建) exam. This would give you systems and information that you normally wouldn't have access to. It also gives you the ability to negotiate more on the listing price, like my friend Kawamura-san did for his family home. I can imagine that it might help with financing as well—banks might feel more confident in a trained professional—but I don't have any experience to say for sure.

To become a real estate broker in Japan, you need to obtain a specific qualification that allows you to perform legal checks and ensure compliance with the law. A real estate business in Japan must have one qualified broker for every five employees. The process to obtain this qualification is as follows:

- Pass the real estate broker examination, which is held in Japanese. The pass rate is approximately 15%, making it challenging for beginners to pass in just one year.
- Register with the prefectural governor once you have successfully passed the examination. All documents and procedures are conducted in Japanese, so language proficiency is essential.
- Obtain a real estate broker certificate issued by the governor. This certificate also involves Japanese documentation and processes.

For those already working in the real estate industry, there's a beneficial "five points exemption" system that allows exemption from certain questions in the real estate exam, effectively lowering the passing line. To use this system, you need to complete a designated course by the Ministry of Land, Infrastructure, Transport, and Tourism, such as the Registration Course for Real-Estate Building. The real estate exam must be taken within three years of passing the course.

Having all the study material for the real estate broker's exam, I'm excited to take on this challenge one day. I have a flexible schedule and a passion for diving into new challenges, and I'm determined to go all-in when the time is right. Though the Japanese language can be daunting, and fluency in Japanese, including all the real estate terms, is necessary to pass the exams and complete all the registration paperwork. I'm already familiar with many kanji characters, as I encounter them daily while browsing property listings.

While the pass rate of 15% may sound discouraging, I've noticed that some of the prominent real estate companies operating in Japan require their employees to take the test annually. As a result, the passing percentage is likely higher when considering the influence of these larger firms' employees, most of them not aiming to pass the test. Surprisingly, many successful real estate brokers and entrepreneurs in Tokyo don't hold this license themselves; instead, they have qualified individuals in their office who possess the certification and sign the final documents for them.

Real Estate Information Network (REINS)

If you do get your real estate agent license, you will be able to access the Japanese Real Estate Information Network (REINS). In 1990, the Japanese Ministry of Land, Infrastructure, Transport, and Tourism (MLTT) launched REINS in accordance with the Real Estate Brokerage Act. REINS serves as an extensive and searchable property database in Japan, overseen by the Japanese government.

Real estate listings are contributed to REINS by licensed realtors, and these listings are then made available to other realtors and real estate brokers. It's important to note that all information on this platform is exclusively provided in the Japanese language and is accessible solely to licensed real estate professionals.

Engaging a real estate broker provides you with access to all the listings available within the REINS database. However, a significant portion, if not the majority, of akiyas and budget-friendly properties may not appear in the database. This is because it might not be deemed worthwhile to go through the effort of listing such properties on REINS. For example, the information for my Tree House property was available on REINS, while my Sangenjaya House was not.

THINGS TO CONSIDER

When assessing a property's potential, I always look at the limiting factors. You can never change the location of a property. You can never change the amount of sunlight shining into the windows in an apartment building in Japan. You can never change the direction of a house. You can never change the year a house was built. If a house is near a noisy highway, or next to a nightclub, you'll also be limited. No matter how much money, beautiful wood, marble, time and love you spend making these places look nice, you can almost never change these limiting factors. In addition to the price, a good location, decent size, and great sunlight are what I always look for when looking for a new renovation project.

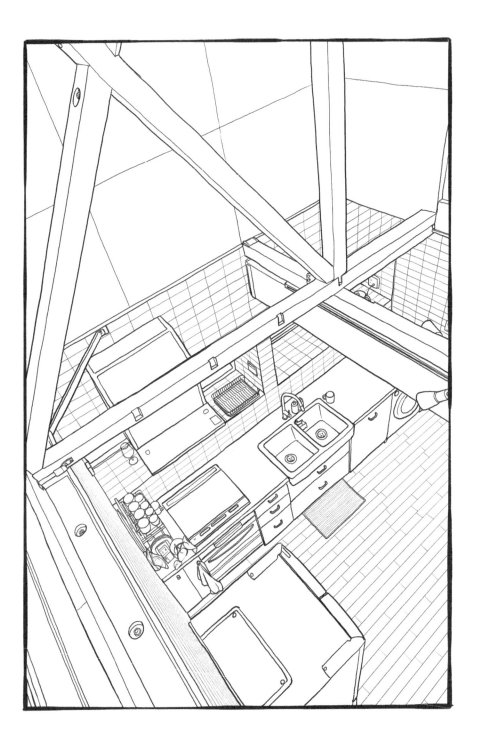

Sunlight

I mention this frequently, so by now you know it is a priority to me. Your priorities may be different, but I would argue that natural light is important to most people. It's just so beautiful, and much nicer than always having to have the lights on. As I've said, you can't really control how much light is available in any given house. It's either there or it's not. Though you may be able to make changes in renovation that affect this. I'll share more about my Sangenjaya House renovation later, but one of the projects in the house was specifically around maximizing sunlight. The earthquake retrofitting for that home meant losing a window on the main floor, making the kitchen very dark. As a countermeasure, I removed the bedroom above the kitchen so that the light from that upstairs room streamed down into the kitchen below. So yes, I did increase the sunlight available in the house, but at a great cost of time and energy, not to mention losing a bedroom in the process! It turned out beautifully, and I love how it looks, but it was a major undertaking and not necessarily something you'd want to do on every house you renovate!

Location

Remember, the real estate saying "location, location, location," matters a lot, even in Japan. Where your property is located can really affect how easy it is to sell in the future. Picking a place that people really like and find convenient usually means it'll keep its value. Before you go ahead and sign that contract, take a step back. Is the property in a good spot for selling later? This isn't just about getting a house—it's about making a smart choice that could make things easier for you later on.

🔑

JIKO BUKKEN

Much of the news that reaches beyond Japan's borders seems to focus on the country's more peculiar cultural aspects. "Rent a girlfriend for a day," kind of news, for example, and people believe this is something every Japanese person does. One such cultural element is the jiko bukken (事故物件). These are properties with unique histories tied to unfortunate events like suicides, murders, or fires. Some people abroad might be familiar with this concept, but it is less-openly discussed within Japanese society due to the cultural beliefs surrounding such properties.

According to traditional Japanese beliefs, all humans have a soul called the reikon (霊魂). Upon death, if the proper ceremonies are held, the reikon joins its ancestors and becomes one of the protectors of the family. This is the spirit that Japanese people honor during the Obon (お盆) Festival in August.

Like many ghost stories of the Western world, if the person experienced a sudden or violent death such as a murder or suicide, or powerful feelings such as jealousy, hatred, or sorrow, the reikon may transform into a yurei (幽霊) and come back to the physical world. It will stay, tied to the place that the tragedy took place, until it can be laid to rest by resolving whatever conflict ties it to the physical plane.

Japanese people tend to avoid living in jiko bukken due to these deeply-ingrained cultural beliefs. Places where tragic events, such as suicides or accidents, have occurred are often considered spiritually impure or cursed. The association with such incidents can evoke feelings of unease and discomfort among potential buyers. Many Japanese people prefer to live in spaces that are free from any negative associations or unpleasant histories.

The Japanese are ***not*** the only people who have negative associations with abandoned houses or houses where tragic events have occurred. This is a world-wide phenomenon. How many times have you seen an old, empty house and immediately thought, "That house must be haunted." Or gotten a shiver or a creepy feeling when you've been told that something tragic happened in a house or building. That unease is universal.

The Japanese take this seriously and Japanese law requires disclosure if anything tragic has happened in a building. There are maps that reveal the locations of jiko bukken. These maps allow home renters and buyers to be sure they are not looking at a property where there may be spiritually toxic residue left behind.

Jiko bukken have piqued the interest of niche companies and investors. As a result, the competition has increased significantly, making them even harder to buy.

I'm not superstitious, but I have never bought a jiko bukken. While they might be cheaper, I believe better opportunities exist elsewhere in the market. It's important to acknowledge their existence but explore other options for the best deals.

Hidden Risks

Sometimes, a property might look great on the outside, but there could be hidden problems. Before you sign, take the time to find out if there are any issues you should know about. This could include legal stuff, like any problems with the property's ownership, or if it follows all the rules for building. Ask your broker to uncover these issues, and I suggest also checking with the municipality.

Before you make that big decision, think about the risks that might come with the property, like natural disasters such as earthquakes or floods. You should check hazard maps to see if the area is prone to these kinds of problems. Also, what are the governments or municipalities plan for this area in the future?

If a natural disaster happens, you'll want to know if you can rebuild your house. Some areas might have rules that make it hard to rebuild after a disaster. This could affect your plans for the future. Is the road in front of the house 2 m (6.5 ft) wide meaning you wouldn't be allowed to rebuild? Unsure? Ask your broker!

Rules & Restrictions

Again, make sure you ask enough questions while you're considering your potential property! Can you do what you want to do? Airbnb licenses are difficult but possible for homes, and nearly impossible for apaatos and manshons. Considering an apartment conversion? Check with the municipality and make sure the zoning allows it.

What about in rural areas, is the home on farmland? Will you be able to run a commercial business in the building? (Spoiler alert: hotels, vacation rentals and Airbnb's are considered commercial businesses.) Whether urban or rural, you might not be allowed to have a hotel or Airbnb in your home if it's against the zoning restrictions, too close to a road, too close to a school, or any other number of things.

In general, if you're going to do anything other than just live in your house, you need to check on the rules. Ask your broker first—they can give you a fair indication. But always check with the municipality before making that final decision.

THE IMPORTANCE OF RELATIONSHIPS

There is an old rundown Chinese restaurant in my area that sells great dumplings, cheap. This small place with about ten to fifteen seats probably hasn't been renovated in about fifty years and still uses an old Japanese "hole in the ground" toilet. The owner of the place, an old talkative man, is always around. He walks slowly, has a long gray ponytail set up in a hairband and jokes with everybody when they enter his restaurant. One day, right before closing time, his friends came in to have a quick chat. Two older Japanese men, laughing a lot, were joking around with the friendly owner while they enjoyed a drink. I overheard some real estate words before they left a few minutes later. After I finished my meal, while paying the check, I asked the dumpling restaurant owner if he was into real estate. The old man's face lit up and he told me about all the buildings in the area he owns and what is for sale. I had met this man probably twenty times before and never knew. He knew about all kinds of deals all over the area—buildings I have never seen through traditional channels or information I would never get in the traditional way.

A few days later I came back to chat with him again and he asked me if I wanted to buy one of his buildings. I politely declined, but every time I see him he tells me about all of the off-market deals going on. I would have never imagined that this guy, running this tiny, rundown Chinese restaurant ten minutes away from Shibuya Crossing was deeply involved with real estate.

This experience reinforced my belief that it's important to spend time with the community you are buying into. If you belong to the community, and give to the community, the community will give back to you.

🔑 7

Buying Your House

You've found your dream Japanese house. It's a wonderful blend of traditional features like blue kawara (かわら) tiles, tatami (たたみ) rooms, and fusuma (ふすま)—sliding doors—in every nook. *(We'll talk more about these features in the next chapter.)* You're set to embark on this exciting project, but buying real estate in Japan can be a bit of a maze. How do you go about it, and what do you need to think about? Can foreigners even get financial help for this?

In this chapter I'll break down the initial costs that come with buying property in Japan and also tackle the world of taxes and expenses you should know about before taking the leap. I'll also share some ways to keep your costs under control including personal stories, tips, and tricks to make your journey smoother.

The intricacies of Japanese real estate can be a head-scratcher, even for native Japanese speakers. As a foreigner making a life in Japan, you'll also encounter your own set of bureaucratic challenges which may often feel like wading through molasses. Based on my experiences, patience, respect, and trust in the process are your allies here.

BUYING SANGENJAYA HOUSE

Acquiring my abandoned Sangenjaya House and transforming it into an internet sensation and an Airbnb success has been an incredible journey that took well over a year—longer if you include the time I spent thinking about the house before I actually started to talk to the owners. It all began when I had purchased Liton House a few years previously in the same neighborhood. As I've shared, I renovated that home and converted it into two charming apartments. I got to know my neighbors, particularly the older Japanese residents who had been living in the area for decades. They taught me a lot, not only about the area but about Japanese culture in general.

Thank you Shimada-san, Sawada-san, Tanaka-san and Hirao-san for always having my back despite my loud renovation work!

One day, one of my neighbors, a kind lady named Sawada-san, pointed out several abandoned houses to me. She had grown up on my street and hoped I would revive more of the homes in her beloved childhood neighborhood. I appreciated the gesture, but I was still so busy with Liton House that I didn't give it much thought at the time. When that renovation was completed, however, I started to get excited about another challenge.

One of the houses that Sawada-san had pointed out to me kept popping up in my mind. I had passed it more than 150 times, always eyeing the facade while trying to picture what it looked like inside. Determined to find the owner, I left notes in the mailbox and attempted to contact them directly. Unfortunately, my efforts proved fruitless, and it seemed impossible to reach the owners. Inquiring with Sawada-san again, I learned that the owners had passed away approximately twelve years ago, but she knew their children. Armed with this information, I obtained the contact details of the owners' children and reached out to them.

Their response was both surprising and cautious. They had been coming by the house about once a month to air it out, and at one point they asked me if I was truly sure about buying the house. A month later, when they came by to air it out again, they granted me a quick tour of the property. Once I stepped inside, I couldn't believe what I was seeing. I was shocked by not only the size of the house and the incredibly steep staircase to the upper floor, but also by the amount of things still in the house—it was brimming with belongings and memories. While I could see that this renovation would be a bit of a challenge, I also knew that there wasn't going to be a better chance at finding a house in this location. I told them I wanted to buy it. It was a crazy decision and I had literally no idea of how huge this project was about to be.

Because I had lived in the area and they had seen the other renovations I had done with Liton house, I had a connection with them, but they were still surprised by my interest. "You want to buy THIS?" I told them yes, but I had no idea when I'd be able to purchase it or for how much. I just knew I wanted the house—the location was (is) amazing, and it would be a great project. I told them I knew a great broker (my friend, Kawamura-san, who I'd helped find his family home). I introduced them to each other.

Months passed.

In early 2021 they came back again to air out the house and I asked them to let me see inside again. The owner explained that the parents had passed away (not in the house) and they had to have all the siblings agree to sell the home. They were waiting for a sister who lives abroad to get the final signature in order to sell the house.

More time passed and I didn't think it was going to happen as I hadn't heard anything. Six months later my broker called and said they were ready to sell.

"How much money do you have?" he asked.

I still didn't know how much they were asking, so I asked, "How much do they want?"

Kawamura-san said, "They only want to sell the house to you, nobody else. So they need to know how much money you have so they know if you can afford it."

Not only did they not know if I could afford it, I didn't either, since I didn't know how much the house was worth. So my broker contacted another local broker and they came up with a valuation for the house. It was a great price, but still a lot more money than I could easily put my hands on.

I went to my parents. I went to my sisters. I pulled together as much money as I could, but it was still only about 60% of the valuation of the house. I figured that was it—there was no way I could afford it and this deal just wasn't going to happen.

But I had underestimated the power of relationships and community. When the owners had said they wanted to sell the house to me and only me, they meant it. We had forged a good relation-

HOME INSPECTIONS

While not required, in the United States it's typical to have a home inspection before purchasing the home.

I have never had a formal home inspection.

No home inspection leads to a smoother transaction, plus you'll have more room for bargaining with the seller. If you have a home inspection done the seller thinks you might be troublesome, making the negotiations more challenging. On the downside, you are responsible for all possible complications so make sure to visit the property and do your own inspection before purchase. Some akiya might be in severe states of disrepair, and the renovation costs could be higher than the property's purchase price.

So, I don't do them, but never say I told you not to. Do your own research, get your own information and make your own decision.

Buyer beware.

ship over the 15 months it took to make this deal happen, and they knew me. They knew I would renovate the house and make it beautiful. They knew I wouldn't complain that the house was old, that I wouldn't ask for any inspections or repairs. Plus I was paying in cash.

They accepted my offer and two weeks later we signed the contracts.

It took another three months to get the keys—Japan is still analog in many ways and Japanese bureaucracy just takes time.

Purchasing the Sangenjaya House was definitely a marathon, not a sprint. Twelve long months of back-and-forths, and numerous moments where I felt like the seller had forgotten all about me, or that the deal would never go through. In the end, it all worked out. My key takeaway from this purchase? Stay calm, stay respectful, and enjoy the ride.

I worked tirelessly on Sangenjaya House. The house was done and ready to operate in about a year after I got the keys. Obtaining the hotel license to be able to rent it out on Airbnb was incredibly difficult. But I did it, and now travelers from all over the world come to stay in my little slice of Tokyo.

RELATIONSHIPS, AGAIN

I've mentioned it a few times in this book already but I don't think I can emphasize enough how important relationships are if you want to be successful at purchasing and renovating homes in Japan. The relationships you establish with neighbors and cultivating a relationship with the people selling the home you want to purchase are extremely beneficial.

When it comes to purchasing a house, one of the most important relationships you'll have is with your broker. In short: you will need a broker. Get a local one, show them respect, and ask them questions.

When buying Sangenjaya House, I didn't talk about money with the owner one single time. I left the money talk completely to Kawamura-san. I met the owner maybe five times, and we talked about fun things every time. The owner and I got along well talking about life in Sweden, tennis, and cultural differences, while my broker did the talking and negotiation with the owner's broker.

Human connections and community have a much bigger impact on life than you might think. I have inherited old tools, kimonos (きもの) and other cool stuff from my neighbors, and yet *they* always thank *me* for taking their gifts, telling me that "the tools are happier" with me. The same goes with old houses in many cases. I stretched my finances to the limit—the amount of money I raised for Sangenjaya House really was all the money I could scrape together—and yet the owner sold it to me at this low price; 60% of the valuation. If the owner likes you and the community accepts you, money has less impact.

OVERVIEW OF THE PROCESS

Buying a house in Japan is somewhat similar to buying a house anywhere else, though there are a few key differences. For example, in the United States, the typical process for buying a house might look something like this:

- You find a house you want to buy, either through listings or your real estate agent.
- With the help of your agent and information about similar properties and their sales prices (comparables or "comps"), you write an offer and put down earnest money—a small amount such as $1,000–$3,000.
- Maybe there's some back-and-forth on price or terms, but you come to an agreement.
- Maybe there's some back-and-forth on inspections and repairs, but you come to an agreement with that. If there are repairs to be done, they get done.

- The title company researches and reports on all of the legal aspects of the title and the sale and prepares all of the sale documents.
- Buyer and seller sell documents at separate times.
- All of the financial transactions happen with the escrow account, mortgage companies, prior loans or liens, or any other financial parties involved.
- The title change is recorded.
- You get the keys.

In Japan the process is essentially the same, with a few key differences:

- Searching for a house is very different—there aren't multiple sources online and many houses are not listed at all, and no previous sales data is available to be able to estimate the value of a house.
- After you submit your offer—called a moshikomi (申し込み)—there's negotiating on price but this includes *you offering less*. If you have a good broker, they will continue to negotiate and you will usually get the house for even less than you offered in the first place.
- The broker is the one who researches the title and prepares all of the legal paperwork, and everyone signs the papers together—buyer and seller (or their representative) and all of the brokers, all at the same time. You also will need to stamp your papers with your personal stamp, called a hanko (はんこ). More on that later in the chapter.
- Rather than earnest money with the initial offer, you would typically put down a deposit of 5–10% of the purchase price when you sign the papers.

- A legal scrivener (notary)—shihō shoshi (司法書士)—comes later to help you register the documents so everything is properly recorded.
- You might get the keys a few days later, but this is highly unusual. Normally you would not get the keys for 1–2 months after signing the documents. (For the Sangenjaya House I didn't get the keys for three months!)

The process isn't entirely different, but it's not exactly the same either. The idea that you continue to negotiate on price after submitting a written offer seems particularly unusual to an American or European home buyer. But things are done differently here. The biggest practical difference, however, is in how you find the properties in the first place. There are not the same central listing websites like in the US or Europe, and a startling amount of real estate deals happen "off-market." Real estate changes hands without ever being officially "listed" with anyone. Relationships are important everywhere, but they are crucially important in Japan. Everything is easier when you know people who trust you and want to work with you. That kind of community strength and loyalty to friends is a key component of how business is done in Japan.

THINGS TO CONSIDER

If you've purchased a property in your home country, I'm guessing you didn't fully understand the contract. Sure, you probably understood the big parts: "You are agreeing to sell your apartment to me for this amount of dollars, and I guarantee you will have the money in your account by this day, and at the same time you promise to give me the keys." But did you understand the fine print in detail?

🔑

NAVIGATING BUREAUCRACY

Navigating bureaucracy in Japan as a foreigner can be both challenging and time-consuming. Here are some of the difficult aspects that I and other foreigners I've spoken to have struggled with.

- **Language Barrier:** Most official documents, forms, and communications are in Japanese. If you are not proficient in the language, it can be challenging to understand the requirements and procedures.
- **Complex Procedures:** Bureaucratic processes in Japan can be intricate and involve multiple steps. Each government office may have its own set of rules and regulations, leading to confusion and delays.
- **Limited English Support:** While larger cities may offer some English support, many local government offices and agencies might not have English-speaking staff, making it difficult to seek assistance.
- **Lengthy Processing Times:** Some bureaucratic processes can take a long time to complete, particularly when dealing with issues related to visas, residency, or property ownership.

- **Documentation Requirements:** Japan often requires a substantial amount of paperwork for various applications and transactions. Missing or incomplete documents can cause delays or even result in rejection.
- **Limited Online Services:** Despite Japan's increasing digitalization, some bureaucratic processes may still require in-person visits and physical paperwork.
- **Cultural Differences:** Understanding and adhering to Japanese cultural norms during bureaucratic interactions can be essential. Politeness, patience, and respect for hierarchy are highly valued.
- **Stricter Rules for Foreigners:** Foreigners may face more stringent requirements than Japanese citizens, especially when applying for certain permits, licenses, rental contracts, or financing.
- **Bureaucratic Silos:** Different government offices may not always communicate well with each other, leading to additional complications when dealing with multiple issues simultaneously.
- **Lack of Flexibility:** Bureaucratic systems often follow strict guidelines, leaving little room for flexibility or exceptions, which can be frustrating for individuals with unique circumstances.

What happens if someone doesn't keep their promise? Legal actions of course, but more specifically, what happens? Sure, the contract was in your native language and you could read it, but you likely didn't understand all the legalese. Now imagine doing the contract in Japanese.

Make sure you do your homework and ask questions. Do you understand everything said and explained to you? Make sure you do! Your broker will help you through the process—in fact they are required to explain everything you are signing to you during the signing appointment. Don't blame them if there were things you didn't understand.

Reading Documents

During the signing, your broker will give you lots of papers to read, and it's really important to understand everything before you agree to anything. Something you don't understand or feel uneasy about? Ask your broker again!

When your broker hands you a bunch of papers, don't just skim through them. These documents have important information about the property and the deal you're making. Take your time to read them carefully and ask questions if you don't understand something. Your broker is there to help you understand, so don't be shy to ask.

Knowing What You're Buying

It is very important to understand the type of property you are purchasing. Are you acquiring the freehold, owning both the house and the land, or is it a leasehold, where you have rights to the property but not the land? While owning the land might offer long-term

HANKO / INKAN

In Japan, the hanko (はんこ), or inkan (いんかん) stamp, holds a significant role in official documents and everyday life. These small, personalized stamps are often required for various transactions, such as signing contracts, opening bank accounts, or receiving packages.

There are many hanko shops where you can purchase your own hanko. There are a wide array of options, each with its unique design and style, and the choice of hanko can be quite personal, reflecting your individual taste and identity.

Once you've selected your preferred hanko, make it official by registering it with the local municipality. You'll receive a certificate as proof of its authenticity, which you'll need for various official transactions.

I remember the day I got my first hanko. I chose a wooden hanko with my name written diagonally on the stamp. It was special to me and I was so happy that I went through a phase of stamping anything and everything people handed to me. For the record, I don't recommend doing that!

One piece of advice—guard your hanko with care. Losing it can lead to significant inconveniences, as your hanko is not just a signature; it's a symbol of your identity in Japan's bureaucracy. Keep it safe. Your hanko will be required for all the documents required in the purchase process.

benefits, leasehold properties can still have their advantages, so it's essential to weigh the pros and cons of each option based on your specific needs and goals.

In addition, check with your broker on the zoning. We talked about this in the last chapter, but it bears repeating. If you are purchasing in a rural area, is the land zoned as farmland? Will you be able to run a commercial business in this building? A hotel, vacation rental, or Airbnb, is considered a commercial business which you might not be able to operate depending on the zoning. Or the property may be too close to a school, or a road, or some other problem. Ask! You can usually get an indication from the broker but I always ask the municipality directly in order to be sure.

Finally, if you are considering selling the property in the future then ask your broker, or do some of your own research, to ensure that you are buying in an area that has positive growth. Also look into re-buildability for your property! If the house is destroyed, can you rebuild? This is a major factor in setting a price for a later sale if that is your intention.

GETTING FINANCING

Financing a property in Japan can present unique challenges for foreigners without Permanent Residency. Banks in Japan generally prefer to lend money to Japanese nationals, making it more difficult for non-residents to secure loans. Additionally, they tend to favor new constructions over older buildings, making it challenging for buyers interested in akiyas to find suitable financing options. They might be willing to lend a substantial sum for a newly constructed house but hesitate to provide half that amount for a home built in the 1990s.

Smaller banks in rural Japan may be more receptive to providing loans to foreign buyers, especially if they have a strong presence in the local community. These banks often have a better understanding of the local market dynamics and might be more willing to accommodate non-resident buyers.

I've found that institutions like SMBC, Star Ginko, SONY Bank, Rakuten, and a smaller bank in Chiba (whose name escapes me) had a more positive outlook on extending larger loans for older properties. *(Links are in the "More Information" chapter.)* However, be prepared for higher interest rates due to the perceived risk of not being Japanese or a permanent resident.

Investment loans and cash purchases are more straightforward options for foreign buyers. Investment loans are specifically designed for real estate investments and might have more lenient terms compared to regular home loans. They usually require a significant down payment and proof of a reliable source of income, and some banks also require you to speak fluent Japanese.

I've taken a unique journey through Tokyo, knocking on the doors of every bank in search of financing for older, less popular properties. Despite having a valid visa, paying taxes, speaking Japanese fluently, and earning a modeling income, securing loans for these older properties wasn't straightforward. I've had to rely on my brokers' trusted connections to secure the best loans.

Brokers, despite their costs, can be your secret allies. They possess hidden strategies that can help you build crucial relationships and navigate the complex world of Japanese real estate. Investing in their services can pay off in the long run, and they will guide you through the entire process, covering everything from hidden fees and taxes.

FEES AND TAXES

I am no expert in taxes, and there is little you can do to change or eliminate them, or even make them lower. Your broker will guide you through the fees and make sure you pay the fees you have to pay, when signing the contract. Unsure of something? Ask the question. Your broker will guide you through the entire process, and it is incredibly important that you trust them, so choose a broker you trust.

Total purchase costs vary a lot depending on the property you are buying. As a general guide, plan for the fees and taxes to be equivalent to 10% of the purchase price. In reality the fees usually don't get this high—but with this in mind you might end up with some extra money that can go into renovating your house. *(The breakdown of fees and taxes are in the sidebar on the next pages.)*

In addition to the listed taxes and fees, if you're looking at purchasing an apartment then there are Management and Repair Fund Fees that vary depending upon the building. It's important to ask how much these fees will be for the apartment you are purchasing. It's also important to understand the financial stability of the building that you're buying an apartment from so you don't get surprised by the building being sold. You'll need to know how to read an annual report in Japanese, or trust the building management, or have a trusted broker who can read and interpret the report for you.

HOW TO SAVE MONEY

There are three primary areas where you can get your costs down:

- Purchase price
- Real estate brokerage fee
- Legal scrivener fee

You can potentially save some money on the mortgage fees as well if you're able to successfully negotiate with the bank. Each bank works differently, and I have never had much leverage or success in negotiating with the banks. If you do, then congratulations! I have a lot to learn from you.

Let's look at each of these areas in detail.

Purchase Price

To make a successful deal and save on the purchase price, timing and negotiation skills are crucial. As the Japanese real estate market has its unique dynamics, understanding the local trends and cultural aspects can significantly impact your negotiation process.

During January to April, the real estate market experiences high activity, making it the peak season for deals. This happens for a few reasons. Many Japanese real estate companies, developers, and property managers, wrap up their financial year by the end of March. So, they are highly motivated to close as many deals as possible by the end of March. Plus, a lot of new college graduates and people changing jobs start working in April when many Japanese companies start their fiscal year.

The rest of the year is considered the "off-season," which surprisingly also offers many potential opportunities to secure better deals. Just like buying an umbrella when it's sunny or ski gear in the summer, taking advantage of the off-season can lead to more favorable prices for property purchases. There may be far fewer options to choose from, however, making it harder to find the right property. This is similar to real estate seasons in the US and Europe.

When dealing with a property that has been listed for less than six months or more there's room for bargaining, but the seller might

FEES & TAXES

Real Estate Acquisition Tax

- 1.5% of the fixed asset tax value of the land
- 3.0% of the fixed asset tax value of the building

Real Estate Registration Tax

- 1.5% of the fixed asset tax value of the land
- 0.3% of the fixed asset tax value of the building
- 0.1% – 0.4% of the value of the mortgage
- This tax is paid upon transfer of ownership

Real Estate Brokerage Fee

- 3% + ¥60,000 (~$415) + consumption tax (10%)
- Seller pays seller's agent 3% of purchase price
- Buyer pays buyer's agent 3% of purchase price, or seller's agent if there is no buyers' agent
- Consumption tax is based on price, fees and commissions, combined

Legal Scrivener Fee

- ¥72,500 - ¥217500 ($500-$1500)

Stamp Tax

- Paid when signing a construction contract, sales contract or mortgage contract. The tax is based on the price indicated in the contract.

Purchase Price	Stamp Tax
¥5–10 million	¥5,000 (~$35)
¥10–50 million	¥10,000 (~$70)
¥50–100 million	¥30,000 (~$207)
¥100–500 million	¥60,000 (~$415)
¥500–1 billion	¥160,000 (~$1103)

Fixed Asset & City Tax

- Fixed asset tax: 1.4% of the base taxation amount
- City tax: 0.3% of the base taxation amount
- Paid annually

Mortgage Fees

- Up to 2.2% of the purchase price

still be firm on their asking price. A well-prepared and respectful negotiation strategy is essential to reach a mutually beneficial agreement.

Engaging a skilled and trusted real estate broker can prove invaluable in navigating the negotiation process. Brokers with expertise in the Japanese market can guide you through the nuances of the local real estate landscape, helping you find opportunities for cost savings and making informed decisions.

Remember, patience and diligence pay off when searching for your dream property in Japan. By considering off-season opportunities and utilizing effective negotiation techniques, you increase your chances of getting a great deal on your next house purchase.

Cash Purchase

Cash purchases can be attractive to Japanese sellers as they offer a faster and more secure transaction process. By buying with cash, foreign buyers eliminate the need for bank approvals and potential complications that may arise during the loan application process. This can give cash buyers more leverage during negotiations, and they may be able to negotiate a lower selling price, often with a discount of at least 10% or more. This is especially true with older houses.

For example, my friend Ito-san recently bought a house for ¥950,000 ($6,550). The house isn't in bad condition, just a lot of things left behind that he will have to deal with. The house was originally on the market for ¥2 million (~$13,800) but he was able to negotiate the price down because he was paying in cash. Plus, as he'd used the broker before and they knew he wouldn't complain about leaky pipes or something broken the way a Japanese buyer would, the broker was able to use that information to negotiate the lower price. This 105m² (1130 ft²) house is in Chiba, about two hours from Tokyo. In comparison, a similar house about two hours from Stockholm would still be ¥7.25 million ($50,000).

Real Estate Brokerage Fee

Saving money on the real estate brokerage fees can be enticing, but it's essential to approach it with caution. When Ito-san bought his ¥950,000 ($6,550) house, the fees were ¥174,000 ($1,200), over 18%, much higher than the 3% + ¥60,000 that is typical. But it was smart of Ito-san to pay these fees. The broker is motivated to show Ito-san the low-price properties he wants because he'll make a decent commission, and the broker more than earns it with his negotiation skills. He was able to negotiate a final purchase price of less than half of the original listing price!

I had my own experience with this that underscores how important these relationships are—and why you might not want to go with the cheapest fees with your broker.

When I was first entering into the world of Japanese real estate, buying the Tree House, I asked Canadian Senpai for a broker with the lowest fees. I was trying to save money and at the time didn't understand how important the broker relationship was. He sent me to a somewhat shady and obscure real estate company in Shibuya. Their Google ratings weren't great, but they offered an incredibly low flat fee of ¥100,000 ($690) for buying and selling properties.

To be clear, Canadian Senpai wasn't trying to steer me wrong— he'd used the same broker several times. But he had years of experience in negotiating and had bought and sold many, many properties.

He knew how to work with this broker and knew how to get the best deals on the properties he was buying.

My limited knowledge and experience in the market became evident during that negotiation process. By choosing this budget broker option, I did save thousands of dollars on the brokerage fee. However, had I opted for a more trustworthy and motivated broker, I might have had a chance to save tens of thousands more in negotiating the purchase price down even more.

In the end I paid ¥14 million ($96,500) for the Tree House plus ¥580,000 ($4,000) in fees including the ¥100,000 ($690) fee from my bargain basement broker. Normally, there would have been some haggling on the purchase price, but this "cheaper" broker didn't do any bargaining. If I had gone with a more trustworthy broker my fees would have been higher but I might have gotten the house for ¥11 million ($75,800).

I learned a valuable lesson—leaving negotiations to the professionals is often the wiser choice. Experienced brokers have in-depth market knowledge, negotiation skills, and a network of contacts that can help you secure the best deals. While I lucked out with my Tree House purchase, I wouldn't recommend this approach to others. Find an experienced broker you can trust. I've told you about my adventures with Kawamura-san, both in finding his family home and his help buying Sangenjaya House. Now that I have this trusted relationship, I would never do it any other way.

I must say, however, that there was one other exceptional agent who went above and beyond, not only negotiating a substantial reduction in the house's price but also guiding me through the loan application process when I faced difficulties securing financing. This is the broker who helped me buy Liton House just before COVID shut everything down in Japan. His expertise and dedication truly earned him his commission, and thanks to him I got financing from a Japanese bank that had previously denied me for a housing loan.

Legal Scrivener

What is a legal scrivener? A scrivener—shihō shoshi (司法書士) in Japanese— is the equivalent of a notary in the United States. In Japan, the broker handles all the legal research and documents like a title officer at a title company would do in the United States. The scrivener notarizes the documents later and makes sure they are recorded properly.

During my real estate ventures, I've had the opportunity to work with different scriveners. For the Tree House, I relied on my broker to handle the scrivener's services, and it all went smoothly without any hiccups. However, during the purchase of Liton House, things took an interesting turn.

My broker introduced me to a scrivener the day before the contract signing. As I reviewed the proposed fee, I had a gut feeling that it might be higher than what I expected. Trusting my instincts, I decided to address my concerns with the scrivener. I politely expressed that the fee seemed a bit steep for the services I required.

To my surprise, the scrivener was understanding and immediately offered me a ¥72,500 ($500) discount without hesitation. It was a moment of realization for me that sometimes a simple question or expression of concern can lead to favorable outcomes. In the end, I was pleased with the reduced fee and the scrivener's willingness to accommodate my needs.

If you don't feel like going with the scrivener your broker provides you with, get multiple quotes from other scriveners. By comparing the fees and services offered, you can make an informed decision and potentially negotiate a better rate.

Where to Focus

While there are multiple ways to lower your costs when purchasing a home, the biggest cost savings is in the purchase price of the home, so that's the best place to focus. Again, working with a trustworthy and experienced broker is key. Remember, when it comes to these cheaper, older houses and apartments, many brokers won't give their best, because their commission is lower compared to the transaction of a new-built house and they just want a quick deal. If you are easy to deal with and take responsibility, the room for a bargain is also huge. I have bargained houses down by 30%, and my friend Isono-san got almost 80% off of an old house he bought a few years ago.

MEETING THE NEIGHBORS

As I've said before, you want to establish good relationships with your neighbors and this starts with bringing them a small gift, or omiyage (お土産), soon after you move in (or take possession) of your new home. Choose something you like, maybe something from your culture such as a box of candy, some cookies, or chocolate—something that will be an exotic treat for your neighbors. Food items are always a good choice. You will want to give a small gift to your next door neighbors, the neighbor across the street from you, and the neighbors on either side of your across-the-street neighbor. Tell them who you are, why you are there and that you have no bad intentions. Say, "yoroshiku onegai shimasu" (よろしくお願いします) when you introduce yourself. It literally means "I'm looking forward to having good relations with you."

Many neighborhoods have homeowner's associations so becoming familiar with the president of the homeowner's association, the kinjo kaichō (近所会長), is important. Even in neighborhoods without a formal homeowner's association there is still usually someone who is considered by everyone to be "in charge." It's usually someone older living in the neighborhood and it's important to make friends with them. Do your research and ask around. If you ask for the kinjo kaichō and there isn't a formal one, most people will still likely refer you to the unnamed boss of the neighborhood. Take them a small gift as well. Be respectful and courteous and you will do well.

Now you get to start the renovation process. Exciting! We'll start that in the next section.

Part 3
RENOVATING

🔑 8

Getting Inspired

When people ask me where I find inspiration for my renovations, I tell them inspiration is all around me. It's a blend of my Scandinavian background, my love of renovation projects, and my love for Japanese architecture and design. Japanese architects are renowned all over the world. While the tear-down culture has its downsides, I must admit it has also been a contributor to the incredible creativity and excellence of Japanese architecture. When you are tearing down and building new buildings all the time, it makes room to try out new ideas.

I've found that the time I've spent here in Japan has influenced me more than I realized. I am seeing things through Japanese eyes instead of my Western ones. I notice all these influences and I bring them into my renovation projects. Japanese architecture is very clean and modern which blends very well with my Scandinavian background and has created a unique aesthetic that works very well here.

TRADITIONAL ELEMENTS IN A JAPANESE HOUSE)

As a foreigner living in Japan, one of the aspects that has captivated me the most about this beautiful country is its unique and rich cultural heritage. The elegance and charm of traditional rooms, adorned with fusuma and tatamis, have left a lasting impression on me. Whether or not you choose to use these things in your renovation, it's good to know what they are.

Fusuma

Fusuma (ふすま) are sliding doors made of wooden frames covered in thick paper or fabric, traditionally used to divide rooms in Japanese homes. These beautiful doors are not just functional but are also works of art, often adorned with intricate hand-painted designs. The beauty of fusuma lies not only in their decorative appeal but also in their practicality, allowing rooms to be opened up or closed off according to different needs.

Tatamis

Tatamis (たたみ) are straw mats, carefully woven and bound with rush grass, creating a soft, natural floor covering. These traditional mats serve as a foundation for various Japanese rooms, evoking a sense of comfort and tranquility. Walking on tatamis feels different from stepping on hardwood or carpeted floors; the experience is gentle and soothing, making it an integral part of the traditional Japanese lifestyle.

Kawara Tiles

Traditionally, kawara (かわら) tiles were the preferred choice for roofing in Japanese houses, showcasing their iconic red color and curved design that added a timeless charm to the architecture. However, in recent years, a shift has been observed towards using tin roofs instead. The reason for this lies in earthquake preparedness.

Japan is prone to seismic activity, and with the potential threat of earthquakes, safety considerations have become a top priority in modern construction and thus fewer new homes built with kawara tiles. Tin roofs are much lighter compared to traditional clay kawara tiles, reducing the overall weight on the house's top structure. This weight reduction minimizes the risk of collapse and damage during seismic events, making it a preferred choice for homeowners seeking added protection and peace of mind.

While the transition to tin roofs is a modern adaptation for earthquake safety, the nostalgic allure of kawara tiles still lingers, adorning traditional homes and heritage structures, a testament to Japan's harmonious blend of time-honored tradition and contemporary innovations.

Tsuchikabe

Tsuchikabe (つちかべ) is a traditional Japanese wall construction method that uses earth and straw to create thick walls, providing excellent insulation and ventilation. The earthy tones and texture of tsuchikabe walls add a rustic and natural feel to traditional Japanese interiors.

Genkan

The genkan (玄関) is the traditional entranceway of Japanese homes. The genkan floor is usually at the ground level, and the rest of the floors in the house are raised slightly, so you step up from the genkan into the house proper. It serves as a space to remove shoes before entering, a custom deeply ingrained in Japanese culture. It is customary to remove shoes but to have on socks or your house slippers when you step out of the genkan and onto the tatami mat floor. No bare feet! And don't step on the edges of the tatami. This is bad manners.

Kotatsu

The kotatsu (こたつ) is a low, heated table covered with a thick blanket. It is a quintessential element of Japanese winter comfort, providing a warm and cozy space for families to gather and stay snug during the colder months.

Tokonoma

The tokonoma (床の間) is an alcove in a traditional Japanese room designed for the display of art, calligraphy, or flower arrangements. It represents a space of honor and aesthetic appreciation.

Engawa

Engawa (縁側/掾側) is a veranda-like space often found in traditional Japanese houses, providing a seamless transition between indoor and outdoor areas. It serves as a place for relaxation and contemplation, offering a close connection with nature.

PRESERVING TRADITION

Despite the enchantment these traditional elements bring, the modern landscape of Japan is evolving, and so are the preferences of homeowners. With changing lifestyles and architectural trends, new-build houses in Japan now tend to opt for more Western-style layouts with carpeted floors and hinged doors. While many foreigners, myself included, find Japanese rooms aesthetically appealing, the demand for such traditional rooms is dwindling in the modern housing market.

Fortunately, there are still pockets of traditional Japan that maintain the use of these elements. In some ryokans (旅館)—traditional inns—and older homes, you can still experience the genuine charm of these classic elements. Additionally, some renovation projects strive to blend the old with the new, creating a unique fusion of traditional and contemporary design.

The changing landscape of Japanese homes doesn't diminish the allure of these traditional elements; rather, it highlights the diversity and adaptability of the culture. Embracing modernity while preserving and cherishing the essence of tradition is a testament to the timeless allure of Japanese aesthetics.

I continue to find myself captivated by the delicate beauty of fusuma, the unique feel of tatamis, and the charm of kawara, tsuchikabe, genkan, kotatsu, tokonoma, and engawa. Yet, I also embrace the evolving architectural landscape, appreciating the fusion of cultures that make Japan an ever-fascinating place to call home. While new-build houses may not commonly feature Japanese rooms, the essence of Japan's rich cultural heritage can still be experienced in various aspects of daily life, reminding me that the beauty of tradition is forever intertwined with the vibrancy of modernity.

JAPANESE CARPENTRY

I absolutely love Japanese miyadaiku (宮大工) carpentry. From my perspective, it is an extraordinary art form that has captivated me since first arriving in Japan. What sets it apart and makes it even more fascinating is the fact that these skilled artisans, also known as miyadaiku, construct remarkable wooden structures without the use of any screws or metal nails. Instead, they rely on ancient joinery techniques that interlock wooden pieces like an intricate puzzle, creating structures of unparalleled strength and beauty. The dedication and precision of miyadaiku craftsmen have left me in awe, and witnessing their masterful work has been an unforgettable experience during my time in Japan.

I had the extraordinary privilege to work with my trusted friend and Japanese carpenter senpai, Kazuki-san, on the Sangenjaya House. He has incredible knowledge and skill with making the types of beautiful cuts that miyadaiku use in their craft.

When I was working on Sangenjaya House I had the very unpleasant experience of finding active, live termites. Lots of them. (I'll tell you that story in Chapter 10.) Some of the primary structural beams had been severely damaged, and at that moment I knew I would not be able to handle the entire renovation on my own; I needed the help of a real carpenter. By this time I had forged a good relationship with the man I call The Lumber Guy at my favorite lumber store, Marubi.

The Lumber Guy introduced me to an older carpenter who came to the house and started working, but I could tell that he didn't quite have the experience needed for the project. He'd ordered a lot of materials that were all wrong, and over a three week period he only did three days of work (which I paid him for) that I knew was going to all have to be redone. I wasn't exactly sure what to do with him, as the project was feeling stalled, so I went back to The Lumber Guy and asked for help.

A few days later, The Lumber Guy called and said, "We have some younger carpenters coming to help, are you home?"

I said, "I'll be there in half an hour!"

Once I got home, the original carpenter was there along with The Lumber Guy, and my new, "younger" carpenters, who were easily in their 50s or 60s. They had already seen the work the original carpenter had been doing and were shaking their heads. The Lumber Guy introduced me to the general contractor, Kaneko-san, and Kaneko-san introduced me to two of his carpenters, Fukamizu-san and Kazuki-san, who would be working on my project. Not only were they easily in their 50s or 60s, Kaneko-san told me that they had 40–50 years of carpentry experience. ***Each.***

They dismissed the original carpenter, right on the spot, and set about fixing all of his problematic work. I think they all felt a little bad that I had gotten into this position and were very concerned about getting everything squared away. I felt a little bad things hadn't worked out with the original carpenter, but he had cost me a lot of time and money, so in the end, it had to be done.

I gave them a few days to work on their own, and then started asking if I could help. At first I would just carry things for them, but soon I was helping them set floor joists and working with them as a team. I loved every minute of working with them and soaking up as much knowledge as I could. We worked side-by-side for a few weeks, putting a concrete slab under the house and retrofitting the entire house for earthquake safety.

At first Fukamizu-san and Kazuki-san were unsure about me helping. They were not used to that. They said I was the only client EVER to help with a project.

When the job was almost done, Kazuki-san asked, "What are you going to do with the staircase?"

You see, I had a vision for Sangenjaya House. I knew that a beautiful, unique staircase would transform it into something truly incredible. But unlike my previous project, the Tree House, this staircase had to ascend a soaring 3.3 meters (10.8 feet) to reach the second floor.

I'd followed the standard Japanese practice of calling in a staircase maker to measure and craft one for me. It was the normal way, but I wasn't very excited about it and hadn't yet given the go-ahead on the project. The estimate had taken a week, instead of the promised 1–2 days, and it was going to be a generic, run-of-the-mill staircase that was going to cost ¥362,500 (~$2,500). No customization, no real wood, just cheap veneer prefab pieces to be assembled on-site in about a day. So it was going to be expensive *and* cheap. Expensive in cost, cheap in quality.

When Kazuki-san asked about it, as we were about to wrap up the project, I was a little startled that he had said anything at all. He is normally very shy and doesn't speak much. But that day, he began to talk. He told me that he had been a carpenter for forty years and had never been allowed to build, to hand-craft, a wooden staircase. He asked—almost begged—me to let him do this.

"Anton," he said, "please let us build this staircase together."

I agreed.

The Lumber Guy (and practically everyone else) thought we were nuts.

Our first step was to order substantial logs of natural Douglas fir. The Lumber Guy said not to.

"Don't do it!" he said, "Building a staircase in natural wood? Is that even possible?"

But Kazuki-san and I were determined. We paid around ¥188,500 (~$1,300) for the wood, which arrived and sat in the house for about a week until the Obon (お盆) holiday festival in the heat of August.

Staring at those logs, imagining them becoming a staircase, felt almost surreal. Kazuki-san decided to dedicate his entire holiday to this project. For six consecutive days, we planed, cut, sanded, measured, laughed, focused, learned, and of course, indulged in plenty of delicious meals. We worked tirelessly in the scorching Tokyo heat, smelling the amazing aroma of the fir wood dust. I absorbed a wealth of knowledge during those days, and Kazuki-san became my Japanese carpentry mentor.

He taught me intricate details about Japanese woodworking, like the precision of shaku (尺) measurements and the art of authentic Japanese carpentry. We handcrafted the handrail and balusters from recycled Swedish oak, my personal favorite wood. However, on the fifth day, after countless hours of work, I made a mistake when installing them. I misjudged the length of the first piece of wood, making the balusters slightly crooked. Surprisingly, no one has ever noticed this error, thanks to Kazuki-san's meticulous craftsmanship.

Completing that staircase filled me with hope and renewed energy. It was a testament to beauty born from dedication and craftsmanship. It took substantially more time to create, but at almost half the cost of the prefab unit. It is truly a work of art—it's featured prominently in the illustration in this chapter. It also marked the turning point for Sangenjaya House after months of demolition, structural work, and cleaning. Kazuki-san later became instrumental in many of the challenging aspects of my Sangenjaya House project, strengthening our bond further.

He became not only my carpentry sensei but also a dear friend, teaching me invaluable insights into Japanese culture and craftsmanship. This journey was a far cry from my fashion industry days, but it was more enriching than I could have ever imagined.

INSTAGRAM

There are great sources of inspiration on Instagram! Here's some of my recent favorites:

@dylaniwakuni: A master of traditional Japanese carpentry, well worth watching. His small school in Kyoto is a place of incredible craftsmanship.

@chantarokichi: More Japanese carpentry.

@japanesethatchingguy: Japanese thatching.

@japanpropertycentral: A beautiful feed of Japanese architecture and real estate from a Tokyo real estate company.

@tokyobuild: Highly detailed miniature models of old run-down Japanese houses, including tiny air conditioner units and windows.

@jeremytsa: Japanese-language content about finance and real estate—a great way to immerse yourself in Japanese real estate and learn the language, too.

@cheaphousesjapan: Great for browsing cheap listings and houses in Japan from abroad.

Check the "More Information" chapter at the end of the book for the full URL's, plus a special URL that will give you 20% off of the newsletter services from @cheaphousesjapan!

In hindsight, choosing the path of crafting our staircase, despite the time it consumed, was the right decision. Those hours spent creating this masterpiece taught me immeasurable lessons, forged lasting connections, and allowed me to proudly say that this staircase is the most beautiful piece of woodwork I've ever crafted. It's a testament to the magic of DIY renovation, an art that has enriched my life beyond measure.

Kazuki-san and I still spend lots of time together. We hang out once or twice a month, or much more frequently when I have a DIY project going on.

INCORPORATING MODERN CONVENIENCES

As you know, I have a strong preference for natural materials and doing things in traditional ways, like I did with Kazuki-san and the staircase. But sometimes modern is the way to go. Design preferences can be a matter of taste, and in my case, I lean towards simplicity. Despite the impressive functionality of Japanese microwaves with their built-in oven features, I had my heart set on a dedicated built-in oven, which I've added to my renovations. Another item I always want to include is a dishwasher. While they're not a common sight in many Japanese homes, I was determined to have one in my Sangenjaya House for the convenience it offers. My vision included a full-sized dishwasher—a necessity in my opinion. However, the only options usually available are smaller drawer types. Finding a full-sized dishwasher turned out to be one of the most expensive investments for my house, costing around ¥232,000 ($1,600). To put things into perspective, this dishwasher was three times the price of the same exact Electrolux model available in Sweden. (Here's a potential business idea for the enterprising minds out there: importing appliances that are both affordable and renovation-friendly for Japan!)

In the realm of kitchen building, my Japanese carpenter friends found it amusing when I mentioned building cabinets. Their approach is refreshingly straightforward: just purchase a ready-made unit and install it. Voila, the job is done! While I might experiment with using a unit in my next renovation project, there are some excellent—and interesting—options available on Yahoo! Auctions. I share more about that in Chapter 11, "Sourcing Building Materials." Meanwhile, the pragmatic mindset of my carpenter friends certainly leaves me contemplating the efficient simplicity they embrace.

Whatever your go-to sources are, I hope that you become influenced and inspired by traditional Japanese elements. Now let's delve into the types of Japanese structures you'll encounter in search of your home. See you in the next chapter.

🔑 9

Understanding Japanese Construction

In the realm of architecture, Japan has been an epicenter of innovation, creativity, and resilience. Its architectural journey is a fascinating tapestry woven with cultural heritage, natural disasters, and visionary architects. From avant-garde skyscrapers in Tokyo's skyline to serene tea houses in Kyoto's gardens, the diversity of architectural expression reflects the nation's rich tapestry of culture, history, and innovation. The nation's unique approach to rebuilding and reinventing spaces has resulted in a thriving architectural landscape that continues to captivate the world. It's worth spending some time sharing both historical context and recent events so you can understand the types of houses and construction you'll find in Japan.

ARCHITECTURE & REBUILDING

Throughout its history, Japan has faced its share of adversity, including devastating earthquakes, fires, and destruction from wars. As a result, the art of rebuilding has become ingrained in the nation's architectural DNA. Time and again, cities and towns have risen from the ashes, embodying the spirit of resilience and adaptability. This constant renewal has shaped a dynamic architectural culture that blends the old with the new.

Modern Japanese architecture celebrates its deep-rooted traditions while embracing modernity. The enduring legacy of Shinto shrines, Buddhist temples, and traditional wooden structures continues to inspire contemporary architects. Elements like tatami mats, shoji screens, and engawa have found their way into modern design, preserving the essence of Japanese aesthetics.

Kengo Kuma: Nature's Advocate

Kengo Kuma's architectural vision and dedication to blending natural elements with modern design has truly inspired me. His work reflects a profound understanding of culture, history, and sustainability, which resonates deeply with my own approach to real estate and property renovation in Japan.

He champions the concept of "sustainable regionalism," blending nature and architecture to create spaces that resonate with their surroundings. Kuma's buildings often employ natural materials like wood and stone, connecting people with the environment and fostering a sense of place.

I have long admired Kengo Kuma's iconic projects, such as the Japan National Stadium and the Tokyo Toilet Art Project, which showcase his creativity and commitment to creating spaces that harmoniously coexist with the environment. His innovative use of wood as a sustainable building material has been particularly influential in shaping my own renovation projects.

I dream of one day inviting Kengo Kuma to visit my work in Japan, to share my passion for revitalizing neglected properties and preserving the essence of traditional Japanese architecture. Having him witness the transformation of old, abandoned houses into beautiful and functional spaces would be an incredible honor and a testament to the enduring allure of Japanese aesthetics.

Despite Japan's rich architectural history, Kuma recently sounded a cautionary note about its future. In a world grappling with environmental challenges, Kuma warns that the country's traditional construction methods are no longer sustainable. Rising demand for resources, urbanization, and climate change demand a paradigm shift in architectural design and construction.

Kengo Kuma's philosophy aligns closely with my values as a real estate investor and renovator, and meeting him would be a dream come true—a chance to discuss our shared vision for sustainable architecture and its impact on the future of Japan's environment.

Tadao Ando: The Master of Concrete

One of Japan's most renowned architects, Tadao Ando, has left an indelible mark on the global architectural landscape. Known for his mastery of concrete, Ando's designs seamlessly integrate nature with minimalist aesthetics. His use of light, shadow, and water elements creates tranquil spaces that evoke a sense of serenity and harmony with the environment.

The self-taught Ando is a household name in Japan and famous throughout the world for his unique, and sometimes challenging, structures. But according to the curator of a massive retrospective of his work that appeared in Tokyo in 2017, Ando believes that architecture is a collaboration between the client, the construction company and the architect, and that homes are still the most fundamental part of his work.[*]

As architects face the call for sustainability, they are also embracing cutting-edge technologies to create more environmentally friendly structures. Advancements in renewable energy, sustainable materials, and smart building systems offer opportunities to design eco-conscious spaces that coexist harmoniously with nature. As Japan navigates the 21st century, architects face the challenge of balancing tradition with sustainability, and heritage with innovation. Creating spaces that respect the past while embracing the future is a delicate dance that will shape Japan's architectural identity in the coming decades.

Japanese architecture is a story of resilience, adaptability, and creativity. From rebuilding after adversity to crafting sustainable designs for the future, the nation's architects have left an indelible mark on the world. Through the visionary works of luminaries like Tadao Ando and Kengo Kuma, Japan's architectural journey continues to evolve, enriching the global architectural tapestry and inspiring generations to come.

BUILDING MATERIALS IN JAPAN

Thanks to all of the innovation in Japanese architecture, building techniques here vary, sometimes offering improvements, other times presenting challenges that demand adaptability and compromise. Building structures reflect a harmonious blend of traditional and

---

[*] "Tadao Ando: The Japanese boxer turned Pritzker Prize winner who buried the Buddha," CNN Style, November 5, 2017, https://www.cnn.com/style/article/tadao-ando-exhibition/index.html

modern construction methods. Over the years, three primary building materials—wood, steel, and steel-reinforced concrete (SRC)---have been extensively used, each offering distinct characteristics, advantages, and disadvantages.

Knowing what a building is made of might seem like a detail that would only matter to the architect or the construction crew. But this detail is important as you begin to train your "renovation brain." I have said that inspiration is all around me because I notice things about the buildings around me. I can look at a building and know whether it is built from wood, or steel, or concrete. And this gets my renovation brain going with all kinds of creative ideas. Like a gardener will notice and name plants as they walk through their neighborhood, once you know about building materials you'll start to notice and name them as you walk through your neighborhood.

You may not immediately get the connection between noticing these things and getting inspired, but it's there. The more you notice, the more creative you will become.

Wood

Wood has been a fundamental building material in Japan for centuries, deeply rooted in its rich cultural heritage. Traditional wooden structures, such as temples, shrines, and tea houses, showcase exquisite craftsmanship and architectural design. Even in modern times, wood remains prevalent, especially in residential construction. Wooden houses offer a warm and inviting atmosphere, and they are often preferred for their natural aesthetics and environmental sustainability. Most smaller houses in Japan are built of wood and if you are looking for a cheap old house to buy, it is most probably made out of wood.

Wood, as a traditional building material in Japan, has several pros and cons:

Pros of Wood

- **Sustainable:** Wood is a renewable resource, making it an environmentally friendly choice for construction projects.
- **Beautiful:** The natural beauty and warmth of wood creates a cozy and inviting ambiance in Japanese homes.
- **Adaptable:** Wood's ability to absorb and release moisture allows it to adjust to different climate conditions, while maintaining its structural integrity.
- **Comfortable:** Wood's humidity-regulating properties contribute to a more comfortable living environment, promoting better indoor air quality.

Cons of Wood

- **Less Durable:** Compared to steel and concrete, wood may have a shorter lifespan and require more frequent maintenance and repairs.
- **Vulnerable to Pests:** Without proper treatment, wood can be susceptible to pests such as termites and wood-boring insects.
- **Vulnerable to Movement:** Wood's expansion and contraction due to humidity changes can cause warping, cracking, or gaps in the structure over time.
- **Degradation:** If not adequately protected or sealed, prolonged exposure to high humidity levels can lead to rot, decay, and insect infestation in wood.

Steel Reinforced Concrete (SRC)

With Japan's modernization in the late 19th and early 20th centuries, reinforced concrete construction gained prominence. Steel reinforced concrete (SRC) structures are known for their strength, durability, and ability to withstand earthquakes. This technology has revolutionized Japan's urban landscape, allowing for taller buildings and skyscrapers. Many commercial, office, and apartment buildings in major cities are constructed using SRC due to its seismic resistance and versatility.

Pros of Steel-Reinforced Concrete

- **Strong and Durable:** Steel-reinforced concrete offers excellent structural strength and durability, making it suitable for various types of construction projects.
- **Fire Resistant:** Concrete's inherent properties provide good fire resistance, enhancing the safety of buildings and structures.
- **Low Maintenance:** Compared to wood, concrete requires less maintenance, reducing long-term upkeep costs.
- **Versatile:** Steel-reinforced concrete can be molded into various shapes and forms, providing architectural flexibility.

Cons of Steel-Reinforced Concrete

- **Environmentally Impactful:** The production of cement, a primary component of concrete, results in significant carbon emissions, contributing to environmental concerns.
- **Heavy:** Concrete's weight can be a limitation in certain construction scenarios, requiring additional engineering considerations for the foundation and support.

- **Vulnerable to Corrosion:** If not adequately protected or maintained, the steel within the concrete can be susceptible to corrosion, leading to structural issues over time.
- **Long Cure Time:** Concrete requires a curing period, which can prolong construction timelines compared to other materials.

Steel

Steel structures have become increasingly popular in Japan, especially in industrial and commercial settings. Steel-framed buildings offer flexibility in design, enabling architects to create open and spacious interiors without the constraints of load-bearing walls. Steel structures are also advantageous for their speed of construction, making them ideal for projects with tight timelines.

Pros of Steel Structures

- **Strong and Durable:** Steel is known for its exceptional strength, making it suitable for constructing large and tall buildings that can withstand various environmental conditions, including earthquakes and strong winds.
- **Light:** Compared to concrete, steel is a much lighter material, resulting in reduced foundation requirements and enabling faster construction.
- **Fast Construction:** Steel structures can be prefabricated off-site, allowing for faster assembly on-site, leading to shorter construction times.
- **Flexible:** Steel's malleability and ductility offer architects and engineers greater freedom in designing unique and innovative structures.

Cons of Steel Structures

- **Cost:** Steel structures can be more expensive to build compared to traditional materials like wood and concrete, especially considering the cost of materials and the skilled labor required for construction.
- **Vulnerable to Corrosion:** While steel can be treated to prevent corrosion, it still requires regular maintenance to ensure its long-term durability.
- **Thermally Conductive:** Steel is a good conductor of heat, which can lead to higher energy consumption for temperature control in the building.
- **Environmentally Impactful:** The production of steel involves significant energy consumption and carbon emissions, contributing to environmental concerns.

JAPANESE MEASUREMENTS

You can't talk about Japanese construction without talking about Japanese measurements. In the realm of Japanese carpentry, tradition and precision intertwine seamlessly. One aspect is the consistent use of the "three shaku" measurement, a practice that harkens back to ancient times. In old houses, you'll notice a fascinating pattern— the distance between pillars is precisely three shaku. This traditional unit, equivalent to approximately 90.9 cm (~35.8 in), continues to be the foundation for many skilled carpenters' work. Despite the modern advancements in construction, seasoned craftsmen still rely on this time-honored measurement, preserving the essence of Japanese carpentry and maintaining the beauty of heritage architecture.

🔑

JAPANESE MEASUREMENTS

Here's a list of traditional Japanese measurements—the shakkanhō (尺貫法)—along with their approximate equivalents in metric and standard system measurements. Traditional Japanese measurements are based on a combination of the shaku (尺) and sun (寸) units, which have been used in Japan for centuries.

- **Tsubo (坪):** ~3.3 m² (35.5 ft²)
- **Tatami (畳):** ~1.91 m x 0.95 m (6 ft 3 in x 3 ft 1 in)
- **Issun (一寸):** one sun, ~3.03 cm (1.2 in)
- **Nissun (二寸):** two suns, ~6.06 cm (2.4 in)
- **Isshaku (一尺):** one shaku, ~30.3 cm (11.9 in or ~1 ft)
- **Nishaku (二尺):** two shakus, ~60.6 cm (23.9 in or ~2 ft)

The tsubo is commonly used for measuring the size of land and houses in Japan.

Tatami mats are common floor coverings in Japanese houses and are often used as a unit of measurement for room sizes.

My Japanese carpenter friend, Kazuki-san, who built my San-genjaya House staircase with me, uses the shaku for his work, and through our collaboration, I've become familiar with all of these measurements. Because the pillars in old Japanese houses are typically spaced three shaku apart it gives many old Japanese houses a similar scale and layout, especially if they were constructed during the same time period.

IMPACT OF 2X4 CONSTRUCTION

The introduction of the 2x4 construction method brought about a significant shift in the way Japanese houses are built. Historically, traditional Japanese construction relied heavily on timber and clay-based techniques, which had been the mainstay for hundreds of years. However, in the second half of the 1970s, a new method emerged, inspired by North American construction practices.

The 2x4 method, also known as "platform frame construction," introduced pre-cut and dimensioned lumber, typically measuring (roughly) two inches by four inches (hence the name). This approach streamlined the building process, allowing for faster construction times and greater flexibility in design. It quickly gained popularity due to its efficiency, cost-effectiveness, and adaptability.

This modern construction style offered advantages that traditional methods couldn't match. The precision of pre-cut lumber allowed for tighter-fitting joints, reducing the risk of air leaks and improving energy efficiency. Additionally, the lighter materials made it easier to handle, leading to quicker assembly and lower labor costs.

As the 2x4 construction method gained traction, it gradually influenced the construction industry, leading to a transformation in building practices across Japan. Many new homes embrace this approach, and the traditional timber frame and clay wall techniques have seen a decline in use.

While the adoption of the 2x4 method has revolutionized the construction industry, traditional Japanese building techniques, such as miyadaiku and other carpentry styles, remain an integral part of the country's architectural heritage. The combination of modern innovation and time-honored craftsmanship continues to shape Japan's diverse and fascinating architectural landscape.

MODERNIZATION OF JAPANESE HOMES

Living and working in Japanese houses has taught me a fascinating story about architectural decisions and weather concerns: Japanese houses are built for hot summers—not for cold winters. People used to mention this, but I only truly understood it once I started renovating. Despite Japan's global reputation for high-tech innovation and cutting-edge design, these older houses can be downright cold during the winter months. During the sweltering summers, the first floors with their traditional earthen walls—tsuchikabe (つちかべ)—work like natural air conditioning. However, they turn cold and icy in the winter, chilling everything around them. The gaps in insulation and the windows with unpredictable drafts have become familiar, especially when Tokyo's winter chill hits, with temperatures around 0 °C (32 °F). Bringing them up to modern insulation standards can be a time-consuming and challenging endeavor, as sourcing materials and obtaining accurate measurements are often not straightforward.

Talking about winter, my own home has its quirks too. Our showers are on the first floor, which is common. It helps avoid damage from water leaks and it's easier to put drainage pipes on the first floor. Every winter, my girlfriend jokingly threatens to leave if I don't address the cold. "Muri, muri, muri!" she says. "This is impossible!" We forget every summer how cold it gets, and then winter comes and the showers are frigid because of the tiles and windows. The windows are not double glazed.

I've taken steps to make it cozier. In my latest project, I added heated floors, extra insulation in the walls and floors, and other modern upgrades. This is my ongoing conversation with these old structures, trying to blend their history with our modern life.

THE FUTURE OF JAPANESE CONSTRUCTION

The question of whether Japan's tear-down-and-build-new culture will persist or evolve in response to growing sustainability concerns and changing demographics is a key discussion topic of modern architecture.

And on a personal note, as I browse listings for houses, I've noticed the affordable ones are likely made of wood, a traditional yet beloved building material in Japan, and my personal preference. Interestingly, in my recent conversations with Japanese builders, I've found that they often prioritize craftsmanship over architectural recognition, emphasizing the artistry of woodwork. Is this the shift to building more wooden structures in Japan? I don't know the answer to that question, but my focus will continue to be on finding and renovating wooden structures.

That's where my passion lies.

Now that you're full of inspiration and knowledge, it's time to start planning your renovation.

🔑 10

Planning Your Renovation

I bought my Sangenjaya House without a thorough inspection. I know that not having an inspection is a higher risk, but I chose not to. In fact, I have never had a home inspection. I'm much more likely to get the house at a good price because the owner knows I won't be troublesome. It's worth it to me to get the house for the best price—or at all, since many houses wouldn't be sold to me if the owners had to deal with inspections or other requests.

After cleaning out the trash in Sangenjaya House, I noticed signs of termites on a beam and in the ceiling. The previous owner had covered these traces with white tape—it looked like maybe the tape had been added many years prior, so I assumed it was just a cosmetic fix. There was also a new, DIY pillar nearby, but I chalked that up to owner quirks.

I knew about the termites.

I just didn't realize how serious they were until I started renovating.

Part of my vision for the renovation of Sangenjaya House was to lower the floors so the ceilings on the first floor would be tall and airy, and I wanted to put a concrete slab under the house to prevent any problems later. It had taken two full, long days of backbreaking labor to dig out dirt by hand to lower the floor for the concrete. I had bagged the dirt up to take outside, and as I was carrying out one of the bags I saw a strange mud wall on the stone foundation of one of the central pillars of the house. When I touched the mud, some of it fell away and I saw a mass of termites moving in a little termite highway going up and down the foundation of the pillar.

I am not usually squeamish, but I admit I was pretty grossed out seeing those little white bastards up close for the first time.*

In Chapter 8 I told you about my incredible experience working with Kazuki-san to build the staircase at Sangenjaya House. What I didn't tell you was that in addition to the carpenters, The Lumber Guy also introduced me to The Termite Guy. No matter what I and the carpenters did to repair the damage, it would be a waste of time if we didn't also get rid of the termites.

The Termite Guy came to the house to survey the situation and give me a quote.

When he saw that I was doing all of the work myself with just a couple of carpenters for help (rather than bringing in a whole crew to do it for me), he said, "This is an old house. I will just teach you what to do so you can save money."

He told me that ten years ago they used strong chemicals and could give a twenty-year warranty, but now, to protect the environ-

---

* There is the URL in the "More Information" chapter to a short video on YouTube of the moments right after I found them.

ment, they used gentler chemicals and only have a five-year warranty. He told me everything I needed to do so that I could do it myself.

He said, "Please don't use your money on us."

Such a nice guy.

Based on his kind guidance, I treated the soil with DIY methods before pouring the new concrete slab. I treated all of the existing wood structure between the ground and a height of one meter (3.2 feet), and set up termite bait stations that release slow-acting poison to eliminate the colony. I managed to do most of the work myself, saving a significant amount of money. The Termite Guy would have cost around ¥300,000 (~$2,070) but his guidance empowered me to handle the termite treatment on my own. I still keep my fingers crossed, but I haven't seen any signs that the termites have returned. Thank goodness.

While each house renovation has its own unique challenges there's a common set of things you'll run across that you should consider when planning your renovation. The good news is that before you start thinking about all the down-and-dirty stuff, you get to envision things like how you use sunlight and space.

SPACE IN JAPAN

There is no space in Japan. It's a fundamental aspect of life here, shaping rules and practices in profound ways. Keep this in mind. When you encounter something in Japan that strikes you as unconventional or different from what you might expect in other countries, there's a good chance it's tied to the scarcity of space. This constraint has a far-reaching impact to daily life in Japan, and understanding this scarcity of space is key to appreciating and navigating Japanese culture and society effectively

My projects are located in the heart of Tokyo, and each of my houses stand on land that is quite compact. Let's consider the land Sangenjaya House sits on—a mere 64 m² (389 ft²). That's an 8 x 8 m (26.25 x 26.25 ft) plot. On this small canvas stands a house. I can almost reach out and touch my neighbor's house through my kitchen window on the first floor. I'm fortunate to have a small garden at the back and about 30 cm (~ 1 ft) of space all around the house. I'd venture to guess that your backyard in Brooklyn might even be more spacious than this! Luckily, each of my neighbors on the south side of each house has their garden alongside my south-facing facade, rather than the wall of their house, so each of my houses gets plenty of sunlight.

SUNLIGHT

Like I mentioned, for the Sangenjaya House I removed an upstairs bedroom in order to create more light. To earthquake proof the first floor I had to cover up one of the windows. I removed a room on the second floor to open it up so now the sunlight streams through from the open space above the kitchen. This made the first floor ten times brighter.

I also bought used windows for ¥14,500 ($100) and installed them in one of the rooms that hadn't had windows previously.

I encourage you to consider how to bring more natural sunlight into any space you're renovating. When I'm viewing an abandoned home I'm always considering the amount of existing sunlight, and how I could bring in more sunlight through the renovation. To me, what makes a house beautiful is the amount of sunlight.

BUILDING PERMITS

I get asked a lot of questions on social media about building permits, building codes and laws regarding earthquakes when it comes to Japanese houses. While you might think that Japan, with a culture of lining up in perfect queues and following the rules, might have strict building codes. This is both true and false. True regarding newly built houses, but when it comes to older houses, not so much.

When I purchased the Liton House I hadn't decided for sure how I was going to renovate the space. It wasn't until after I bought the house that I got inspired by the idea of creating two separate living spaces—an apartment conversion. I would live in one part of the house, and the other part would be a completely separate apartment with its own bathroom and kitchen that I could rent out; a great way to help pay the mortgage on the property.

I checked with the municipality to make sure that type of conversion was allowed, but then COVID shut everything down before I was able to get the required permits. I decided not to wait and finished the renovation during COVID. Once things reopened I worked with the municipality and got all the required permits and approvals. If you plan doing an apartment conversion I recommend checking with the municipality first before buying the house, and I would also recommend you get your permits before you complete any renovations. In my experience, the municipalities are encouraging people reviving old homes and will want to work with you, but it's always better to do things in the proper order. There's no guarantee that they will give you the permits retroactively like they did with me.

Japan has strict rules, but during the housing boom (and then bubble) of the 60s, 70s and 80s, there was rampant unpermitted renovation happening. Many homes were expanded and not registered with the municipality. Sangenjaya House was built in 1936 and registered with the municipality as a one-story, 36 m² (387 ft²) house. By the time I was looking to purchase the house it was a two-story, 90 m² (969 ft²), with 45 m² (484 ft²) per floor. It had clearly been expanded, possibly more than once.

I knew this before buying the house but I wasn't going to pull any claims and told the owners that I would deal with all of those issues myself. This is part of why I was able to get the property so cheaply.

After I got the keys I went to the municipality and asked, "How can I fix this?"

They were very, very helpful—they really wanted to help me get things corrected. They sent me to a surveyor who resurveyed the house so the registration could be updated. I paid ¥115,000 ($795) for this. The municipality also asked for pictures of the house for tax purposes. They could have re-assessed the value of the property, but since the structure was so old they didn't change its assessed value—a win for me!

It wasn't just good citizenship on my part that I worked so hard to get all of this corrected. I knew it would all have to be in order with the municipality in order for me to get my hotel license and operate my Airbnb. I was very grateful that things worked out so smoothly.

In my experience the municipality is very open to working with you to resolve any issues, and are very motivated to work with you. You are reviving and renovating one more abandoned house, helping to revitalize the area.

As long as you don't change the exterior, add a floor, or upset your neighbors, you likely don't need permits doing simple renovations in a house. Document your renovation process with pictures to show people at the municipality. That way you can show them what the house looked like when you bought it, which may be different than what they have on record. Plus it's fun to have those before-and-after shots for sharing with friends, too.

BUILDING CODES AND REGULATIONS

There are two key regulations about building size in Japan that are important to know: yosekiritsu（ 容積率 ）and kenpeiritsu（ 建坪率 ）. Yosekiritsu is how much usable floorspace you can have on your property, and kenpeiritsu is how much of your property can be covered by the building. They are different measures but work together. I'll explain.

Yosekiritsu

This is how much usable floor space can be available in the buildings on your land. Not the size of the building itself, but the usable floor space that the building contains. It's expressed as a percentage as compared to the size of the property. For example, if your building has many floors, the percentage of usable floor space compared to the property might be very high. For example, let's say you have a four-story building with 25 m² (269 ft²) per floor. That means you have 100 m² (1,076 ft²) of total usable floorspace in your building. If your land is 50 m² (538 ft²), then your yosekiritsu is 200% (twice as much floorspace as land). Make sense?

Crowded areas such as cities usually have higher yosekiritsu limits, while suburbs have lower ones. In Tokyo, the highest yosekiritsu is 1300% for commercial zones near Tokyo Station. Some buildings even go higher with special permissions.

If you're going to calculate the yosekiritsu for your building, consult an architect for accurate numbers. Basements and small garages might not fully count.

Kenpeiritsu

The second regulation is kenpeiritsu (建坪率), which is how much of your land can be covered by the building. This ensures that some open ground is maintained in every area (important for many reasons, including the drainage of surface water). Back to our previous example, let's say your land is 50 m² (538 ft²) and kenpeiritsu for your area is 50% then your building can take up to 25 m² (269 ft²) of the property.

Since this is a book about old houses, there is most likely already a structure on your land. Even if the previous owner didn't follow these regulations, you'll be okay. I have never heard about a case where people have gotten into trouble for buying something where the previous owner didn't follow the building regulations. People at the municipality have always helped me re-register my old buildings for a small fee after I've invited them to visit. I always enjoy bringing these people over. They always look so excited and surprised at the same time, "Wow, this house is old but it still is cool," they say as they take their measurements and check their boxes on their sheets.

EARTHQUAKE STANDARDS

In Tokyo, every other house looks different, and sometimes you'll come across some crazy looking house with a round tower that was built in the bubble era. While Japanese laws can be strict and people follow the rules, building codes seem less strict compared to a country like Sweden, for example, except for earthquake regulations.

With earthquake regulations, they are very strict. In 1981, a significant change was introduced in Japan's construction standards known as the shin-taishin (新耐震) or New Earthquake Resistant Building Standard Amendment. This amendment was prompted by the destruction caused by the 1978 Miyagi Earthquake. This magnitude 7.4 earthquake destroyed over 1,100 houses and severely damaged another 5,500 houses within the Miyagi prefecture. This is why buildings constructed before 1981 generally tend to be less expensive—less expensive because the banks might not give you a loan

Speaking of strict rules, something that often bewilders newcomers to Tokyo is the stern enforcement of parking rules for bicycles. In many Western cities, you might think nothing of locking your bike to a lamppost or rail near the closest subway station. However, in Japan, this would be considered illegal parking. Enter the "Bike Pounders," a unique profession in Japan. These individuals patrol the streets, cutting locks and transporting wrongly parked bicycles to storage facilities in the suburbs. To reclaim your bicycle, you're looking at a ¥3000 ($20) fee. I've had my bicycle towed away on several occasions. I've never invested in an expensive lock for my bicycle, mainly because I'd rather not have to replace it if it gets impounded again. This works for me because Tokyo is remarkably safe and I don't have to fret about bicycle thieves.

for these pre-earthquake-building-standards structures. Do your research, find out about the appropriate earthquake construction and retrofitting standards and work with an expert to make sure that the buildings you renovate are safe.

TERMITES

If you find termites in one spot, you can be sure they are ***everywhere*** within 100 m² (1076 ft²). That's 10 m (32.8 ft) in any direction. With how closely spaced houses are in Tokyo, this is another reason why neighbors are not excited about abandoned houses; no one is making sure the termites are being treated. I mentioned the termites I found in Sangenjaya House. With that experience I learned some things about termites. Turns out there are two primary types of termites in Japan, Japanese termites and formosan termites.

While having either type of termite isn't ideal, the formosan termite is the worst. Nicknamed the "super-termite," it's more aggressive and difficult to control, and it consumes wood at a more rapid rate than other termites. A colony of formosan termites can chew through about 15 cm (5.9 in) worth of a 2x4 ***every day***. It can also climb higher, so if you have them in the ceiling or up high in the house then you probably have formosan termites. These are nothing to be blasé about. Get help, get it now.

ASBESTOS

Asbestos, a hazardous mineral once commonly used in building materials, poses significant health risks if not properly managed. While I've been fortunate enough to avoid encountering asbestos in any of my own projects, it's crucial to be aware of its potential presence when assessing properties.

Asbestos was widely used in construction due to its fire-resistant and insulating properties. However, its harmful effects on human health, including causing serious respiratory diseases and cancer, led to its gradual ban in many countries. In Japan, asbestos use began to decline in the 1970s, and it was officially banned in new construction materials by the mid-2000s. I am sure I have inhaled a lot of bad things while demolishing and doing renovation, but to the best of my knowledge I have never encountered asbestos. I would never acquire a house knowing it contains asbestos, no matter how cheap it is.

As with so many things in DIY renovation—do your research, know the signs, and get help from a professional if you have any doubts. Like termites, asbestos is not something to mess around with.

ELECTRICAL, PLUMBING, AND STRUCTURAL ELEMENTS

There are three things you *cannot* do in your house: electrical, plumbing, and structural elements.

Electrical

I always leave electrical work to the experts—it's not legal for me to do here, but it's not something I would dabble in anyway. I've enjoyed collaborating with my local electrician, Hashimoto-san, however. We got connected through my community's tatami maker, Namigai-san. Sometimes Hashimoto-san's junior assistant, Satou-kun, would tag along to learn the ropes. Hashimoto-san not only completed all of the electrical tasks at Sangenjaya House but also made sure everything was in line with my hotel licenses. The house still had old knob-and-tube wiring when I bought it so the entire home had to be redone. It didn't cost me a fortune, and I learned a lot from him.

In Japan, the plugs for electrical devices are like those in North America, and the main voltage is 100V. But there's a twist—the frequency of electric current differs in Eastern and Western Japan. It's 50 Hertz in the east (places like Tokyo) and 60 Hertz in the west (like Osaka). It's a bit like the elevator etiquette differences between Tokyo and Osaka—different sides for standing and passing. Always know the area you are in! There may be little differences that you will need to know or remember.

Plumbing

When it comes to water-related stuff, I stay away. Water leaks and mold are just not my thing. I steer clear of plumbing tasks. I recommend hiring professional plumbers to do all the plumbing renovation work. If you do it incorrectly, you might not only create messy problems with blockages or flow issues, you may create a slow, hidden leak that will destroy your house from the inside out.

Structural Elements

When it comes to earthquake safety, adding braces to key areas, or moving or changing walls and structural pillars, I don't take the plunge on my own. A mistake here could literally cause your house to fall down, potentially on top of you, so treat it seriously. Get help from a professional carpenter before changing any structural elements, and be sure to get help with earthquake retrofitting, too.

This is one advantage to working within existing structures like manshon buildings. Sure, you might have to deal with some management company formalities, but the risk of making big mistakes is lower. If you're renovating your own house, the buck stops with you. Remember my advice—before you start tearing down walls or making big changes, consult a pro. It's the safe and smart way to go.

We'll talk more about working with contractors in the chapter on "Navigating Your Renovation."

RENOVATION GRANTS AND SUBSIDIES

Enough hard news. Let's dive into something more fun. Recently, local municipalities in Japan have been on a mission to support homeowners turning old, energy-inefficient buildings into eco-friendly gems. That old Japanese house you're eyeing probably isn't exactly top-tier when it comes to insulation and windows. It's no one's fault as energy standards have evolved over time. But here's the fun part—you could be eligible for some serious financial aid to fix these issues.

Think double-glazed windows, insulation upgrades, and other improvements that'll trim your energy bills and reduce your environmental footprint. There are renovation grants and subsidies now that you can apply for and use to pay for these things. Sounds great, right? The availability and criteria for these subsidies can vary by area, so talk to your local experts to find out what's available. Start with your broker, but also ask your municipality and any of your local carpenters or other tradespeople. They often have the inside scoop from people renovating their old homes with these subsidies.

Builders also have compelling reasons to assist you in obtaining these subsidies because it means more work for them. You save money and they get to help you with your project. Plus, they can often leverage government incentives meant for eco-friendly projects. It's a win-win, and builders are often motivated to guide you through the subsidy application process.

These grants can be quite generous, sometimes even surpassing the amount you paid for your budget-friendly house, with amounts up to ¥5 million (~$34,000). Reach out to your community and explore the possibility. You could turn your old Japanese home into a warm, green haven and save money on energy bills, too.

GETTING CLEAN AGAIN

Cleanliness is very important in Japan, and renovation dirt is the dirtiest dirt there is. It gets under your nails, in your pores, and there's really no way to get it all clean unless you soak, and soak, and soak. For me this is especially important because of my day job. To get clean enough after doing a full day of renovation, I have to go to a local sento (銭湯), a Japanese communal bathhouse, to get clean again. I usually soak for an hour just to get all the paint off and the dirt out from under my fingernails. I could never get this clean in my own bathtub. Even as deep as it is, it's not really big enough for me to get submerged enough to get completely clean. And I need to get completely clean, because tomorrow I have a job.

I have to get married.

Weddings are a huge business in Japan. It's a billion dollar industry, and getting married is the biggest dream for many (if not most) Japanese people. In any convenience store, and convenience stores are everywhere, they have tons of bridal magazines. Zexy is the most famous with five-hundred pages exclusively of wedding content. Wedding dresses, wedding venues, destination wedding ideas, wedding style guides, floral plans, planning guides, reception ideas, music, food, colors, rings, and where to go on your honeymoon—you name it, if it's somehow related to getting married, it's in there. A new issue is released every month, and there is a different edition for each area of Japan. If you look closely at the cover of one of those bridal magazines and you see a photo of a white guy getting married, well, it might be me.

I "get married" for a living.

For real, you must think?

For real.

All those wedding venues that are in all of those wedding magazines? They need beautiful new photos every season showing how gorgeous your wedding will be if you get married there. So they hire me (and several other people) to come and pretend to get married for the camera. We basically simulate an entire wedding with guests, food, music, and laughter for two whole days. Wild, right?

My first ever wedding job was in Yokohama just outside of Tokyo. A two-day advertising job for a wedding venue called Art Grace. To give you some perspective, to get married for real at Art Grace is going to set you back about ¥7.25 million ($50,000).

This was my second time coming to Japan and I could speak little to

no Japanese, making me happy but a bit anxious when my manager told me I booked my first big wedding job.

"Take care of her well," my manager Maeda-san told me while laughing and handing me my job details. The paperwork said that my wife for the day was an experienced Japanese female model from my agency named Maiko. I just kept thinking, "Am I really doing modeling or is this some kind of escort business?!?"

I felt incredibly confused but still curious what this job was all about. This was five years ago, and I have been "married" on set about fifty times since then, but I still remember it as if it was yesterday.

I arrived at the wedding venue in Yokohama early morning after a forty-five minute train ride from Tokyo. The venue was this huge rose-smelling, Disneyesque chapel. I had my own backstage room and got my hair and make up done. Maiko had her dressing room right next to mine. Eguchi-san made us look like newlyweds, dressing her in a big, white wedding gown, and me in a black wedding tuxedo before heading out to different shooting locations at the wedding venue.

At the first shooting location in the chapel, about fifty models and actors showed up. My "dad," my "mum," Maiko's "bridesmaids," my "best men," a priest, a pianist, and about twenty of our closest "friends" to sit in the audience and cheer for us. All of this in a brand new Euro-Disneyesque-style chapel in Japan.

It sounds crazy, and I have a hard time explaining to people what I do for a living without making it sound like a joke. I get paid to get married to a beautiful woman, laugh all day, and eat great food! The days are long but fun, and I love my wedding jobs.

While I might have some kind of world record for the number of times I've "gotten married," my parents back home in Sweden never got married, making this story even funnier. (Contrary to the US, it's not assumed that couples will get married in Europe, even if they are lifetime partners.)

I love my job doing wedding shoots, it is a lot of fun, but I do not see the value in getting married in a shiny, new chapel. Maybe I am jaded from the countless number of times I have posed as a groom, but I recall feeling this way even that first time in Yokohama. In Sweden, the chapels and wedding venues are old, refurbished, or held in nature close to the sea. The buildings have charm, character and history. It would be unthinkable, to me, to have a wedding in a newly built chapel.

Thinking back, I think my wedding jobs were when I really understood how important New is in Japan.

For me, even after five years of living in Japan and continually seeing things more and more with Japanese eyes, I still prefer the older buildings.

They have soul.

Renovating in Japan, especially in densely populated urban areas like Tokyo, comes with its unique set of challenges and opportunities. Understanding the building regulations, documenting your progress, addressing potential issues like termites and asbestos, and knowing when to consult experts are essential elements for a successful renovation project.

Renovating a house is an extensive task, but in most cases, you're the sole owner of the land, allowing for greater freedom. Especially in rural areas, you might have a small garden and space to manage your potential waste (we'll talk about that in an upcoming chapter). Renovating an apartment is relatively straightforward since the structure is already in place. However, you do need various permits from the building management before you can start working on your place. Generally, the newer the building, the more meticulous the people are, and the stricter the building management is about granting these permits. They're also responsible for maintaining the building, including cleaning and fixing things in shared areas. But, ultimately, most people want to help you make something nice out of a neglected property. If you are respectful and known for being someone who contributes to the community, you will probably find that you can do the thing you want to do.

Despite these challenges, renovating in Japan allows you to breathe new life into historical structures and contribute to the preservation of the country's architectural heritage. It's a rewarding journey that combines creativity, culture, and craftsmanship in a truly unique way. Now, you're going to need some materials to get that renovation going. We'll talk about that next.

🔑 11

Sourcing Building Materials

During any renovation project, finding building materials, appliances, light fixtures and other items can be both one of the best and most challenging parts of the DIY adventure.

Reusing items that already exist in the house is one method I use, but I also use reclaimed items I find through multiple different sources. At this point it's worthwhile to talk about "used stuff in Japan," as the dynamic for used items in Japan is quite different from my experiences in the US or Europe.

USED STUFF IN JAPAN

It costs money to get rid of things in Tokyo. A bed? Might cost you ¥7250 ($50) to get rid of. A fridge? About ¥7250 ($50). A chair? ¥1,450 ($10). This, in combination with the obsession of New and the lack of space in Tokyo, contributes to the situation here.

Let's say you buy a kitchen table for ¥29,000 ($200) at IKEA. You use it for a year or two, then you decide to move to a new apartment in a different neighborhood. Your table doesn't work in your new apartment, so you have to get rid of it. The table is still in good condition and you put it out for sale for ¥7,250 ($50) about two weeks before you are moving out—just like you would in the US or Europe—but here in Japan, no one wants to buy it from you. It's a few days before your move and you need to get rid of the table ASAP, you start to panic and call the municipality to order large-sized-waste disposal. They tell you they can take the table for you, but it will cost you ¥4,350 ($30) and you have to wait three weeks. You are moving out in *three days*?! What should you do?!

You give it away.

The table that in your home country would have easily sold for ¥7,250 ($50)—here in Japan you have to give it away for free? Yes. It's faster and easier than dealing with the municipality and paying money for it. Okay, you *might* be able to get some money for that table if you sell it here, but it will take a lot of time, energy and hassle. Way more than the few bucks you'll get for it. You might spend weeks trying to get someone to look at the table, or have to put it on a Yahoo! Auctions and pay fees and freight. Meanwhile the table is taking up space in your home and your life. Better to just let it go.

"FREE!" always attracts people, including you. Thank you for buying my book with this title: *Free Houses in Japan*. I'm glad the title caught your eye, and I hope you are finding the book valuable. Don't discount the power of the word "free."

I have given away bath tubs, bulky and heavy toilets, tables, wood, chairs, beds, fridges, building materials, you name it. I always put things up for free. Once I had two big blue toilets, about 50 kg (110 lb) each, with built-in sinks on the tops of the tanks (this is common in Japan). A guy wanted them because the sink on his toilet had broken and he really just wanted the tops. But they were free so I was able to say, no, if you want them you have to take them both in entirety.

Another time I had a bidet attachment that I could have sold for about ¥7,250 ($50), but it was just easier to give it away for free.

This is the way to get rid of your not-so-expensive things in Japan. First check with your friends to see if they want them. If not, put them up on Craigslist or in any of the Facebook Groups I mention later in this chapter. I always recommend people and friends leaving Tokyo to give away their things for free, unless it is luxurious or special, or it's small enough not to be a bother while you are trying to sell it.

We've talked about how the Japanese prefer **New**. Because of this unique mindset, used items in Japan tend to have lower prices, making vintage and second-hand goods very affordable. This, combined with how well Japanese people care for their belongings (except their houses), has created fantastic deals in Tokyo's vintage market. Similar to how Japanese buyers travel abroad to buy American vintage items in bulk and bring them back to sell here in Japan, there is definitely an opportunity to buy vintage items here in Japan and sell them in the US or Europe, but I'll save that idea for another time.

Japan boasts one of the best second-hand markets in the world. From clothes and designer shoes to watches and handbags, you can find top-notch items that often look brand new. And they're affordable, not just due to the weak yen. Personally, I love hunting for used treasures. I once found a Bang & Olufsen television, an old design piece that would normally be ~¥2.2 million ($15,000), but I got it for ¥7,250 ($50). This plasma television was only ever used as a display model in a showroom, a real relic, but very cool, very beautiful, and it has a great picture. It now lives in Sangenjaya House where my Airbnb guests can enjoy it while they stay.

Unlike some other places, Tokyoites take great care of their belongings, especially clothes. I've seen well-off individuals in other countries sporting ripped jeans and tattered shirts, but not in Tokyo. The Japanese take fashion very seriously. When it's time to declutter their very small apartments, they consign or donate their items to one of the countless vintage stores all around Japan. These vintage stores are great places to find items for your renovation projects.

This careful approach to belongings is linked to Japan's fascination with *New* things—because they prefer *New*, they take great care to make sure that their things always look as *New* as possible. It's also why there are so many like-new clothes and handbags in all of the second-hand markets. For a fashion-conscious Tokyoite, even though they've cared for that item to keep it looking *New*, once it gets to be a certain age, it's old and outdated. Time to upgrade. This careful care is a wonderful trait—the culture of maintenance. But it makes me wonder, why doesn't this apply to Japanese houses? And what about sustainability? We avoid plastic and use eco-bags while shopping, but when it comes to houses, we often tear them down after just thirty years to build something new. It's a paradox that highlights the need for change in my opinion.

Besides vintage stores, and finding things for free there are a few other places I recommend you should use to find materials for your renovation projects.

YAHOO! AUCTIONS

In Japan, people usually prefer shiny new houses over fixing up old ones. But guess what? There's a golden opportunity here that not many know about—a chance for smart folks like me (and you) to snag top-notch stuff like fancy Cucina, Miele, TOTO, and other name brand goodies at bargain prices.

Here's the deal: upscale home builders put up super cool houses to flaunt their skills. These places are like showcases. As time goes on, these houses need a makeover, and that means they get rid of their "old" stuff—kitchens, windows, even posh furniture—and put them up for sale. Many of these items end up on Yahoo! Auctions, which is still available here in Japan.*

It takes a little time and effort to sift through all the listings, but it's so worth it. I've gotten some seriously awesome deals by diving into these auctions. And guess what? Every single thing I've gotten has been in top-notch shape. Shipping charges can be a bit more, but considering the savings and quality, it's a smart move.

Let me share a personal story: for my Sangenjaya House, I scored a set of totally brand-new, high-quality windows for just ¥43,500 ($300). These windows, normally priced at a whopping ¥290,000 ($2,000) each, are now a star feature in this house. If you've got some

---

* The URL for Yahoo! Auctions is in the "More Information" chapter at the end of this book.

wiggle room in your budget and a bit of DIY spirit, you can totally make your dream home shine without breaking the bank. Search for model room exhibits—moderurumu tenji-hin (モデルルーム 展示品)—and then your keyword: kitchen, furniture, bathroom, you name it. You'll find everything. But please don't steal my future deals!

RECLAIM & REUSE

I often source items for my houses by reclaiming and reusing things that are already in the house. For example, in my Sangenjaya house I repurposed some lamps. I had to have the wiring redone in the entire house to replace the original knob and tube wiring from 1936. There were some light fixtures in the bedrooms upstairs from the 70s: plastic, orange, and awesome. I took them down, cleaned them, put in new light bulbs, the electrician wired them up, and presto! New lighting. My Japanese friends think they are tacky, but I love them and think they really fit the style.

I also used this method in the shower and tub area of the bathroom. I put in an outdoor shower area (I'll tell you about that next), but the indoor bathroom was in perfectly good condition. It had a fairly old bathtub, but the entire bathroom was tiled in vintage pink tiles that looked brand new. I'm guessing these tiles weren't original, but were added by the previous owners sometime in the 60s They were so pristine, I wanted to save them. (You can see them on the house tour on YouTube—the URL is in the "More Information" chapter.) The tub was fairly worn and could probably have been replaced, but if I had replaced the bathtub I would have had to retile the bathroom and all of those vintage tiles would have been lost. Instead I resurfaced the bathtub with a Rustoleum Tub & Tile Refinishing Kit that I had to special order from the United States.*

It's so sad to me how the normal approach would have been to just tear this all out and put in a modern molded-plastic bathroom unit kit. The existing bathroom was in perfect condition, and still beautiful. I decided to save it as a way to show people that it is possible for something old to still have value and beauty.

I hope that these kinds of projects demonstrate to people that it's not only possible to renovate in Japan, but that if you already own one of these homes, that it's possible to make something cool out of something old.

SPECIALTY WEBSITES

Sometimes you need something very specific and you just have to order it online. For my outdoor garden space at Sangenjaya House, I needed a Japanese-style bathtub—ofuro (お風呂). Ofuro means "bath" in Japanese, and the type of wooden tub that I wanted is usually found in the sento, the public bathhouse (銭湯). Usually they are indoors, but if you are lucky, they will have the tubs outside. When the tub is outside, it is called a rotenburo (露天風呂), an outdoor bath. In the mountains outside of Nagano (長野市) or Hokkaido (北海道) they have large outdoor areas with baths filled from the natural hot springs in the area and you can have a bath under the stars.

I wanted one for my outdoor oasis.

I didn't have the skills to build one, and to have a carpenter craft one for me would have cost more than the entire renovation, even with the "friends-and-family-and-I'll-work-with-you" discount. So

---

* The refinishing kit info is in the "More Information" chapter at the end of the book.

§

FACEBOOK GROUPS

I really wish I had stumbled upon Building and Renovating a House in Japan back when I first started my renovation journey. It's a fantastic Facebook Group where both newbies and seasoned pros swap their best tips and tricks. We discuss everything from challenges to where to find the best materials, all from the perspective of fellow foreigners navigating the Japanese renovation landscape. Plus lots of those "Can you believe this?" kind of stories.

I'm pretty active on social media, but this group is a whole other level. Need advice on renovation companies or a reliable plumber? Looking for step-by-step guides? This group has got you covered. It's basically a hub for all things related to building and renovating homes in Japan.

If you're looking for more expat connections, Tokyo Expat Network is another great group where you can learn from the challenges and experiences of other foreigners. Plus, keep an eye on various "Sayonara Sales" groups—you might just snag some incredible deals on pre-loved items. These groups are where you can tap into a wealth of shared wisdom and camaraderie.

URLs for the groups mentioned here are in Chapter 19, "More Information."

I ordered one from a specialty website and had it shipped to me. A little expensive, yes, but worth it for the result.

I don't remember exactly which website I ordered the tub from for Sangenjaya House, but I found a website with similar-looking tubs that I've put in the "More Information" chapter at the end of the book.

HOME CENTERS

In Japan, home centers play a significant role in meeting the needs of homeowners and DIY enthusiasts alike. These stores are a treasure trove of various construction materials, tools, and household goods, making them essential for anyone embarking on a renovation project. New home centers are sprouting up in central locations, and more Japanese individuals are developing a keen interest in investing in and renovating older Japanese houses. From a sustainability perspective, this is fantastic news.

One thing to keep in mind is that while home centers offer a vast array of items, the quality of certain materials may not always be ideal, especially when it comes to graded wood. Graded wood, particularly the kinds used for building purposes, requires a specific grade to ensure its suitability and structural integrity. In Japan, many carpenter friends have shared their insights, revealing that home centers often stock B- and C-grade assortments of wood, which might not be the best choice for critical construction projects. Having learned from my own experiences, I advise caution when purchasing white wood (softwood) from Japanese home centers. Often, the wood can be improperly stored, leading to warping even before it's sold. To ensure better quality materials for your projects, consider seeking advice from experts and asking questions before making any purchases.

When it comes to building grade wood, it's advisable to order from local lumber suppliers or places known for their expertise in providing quality materials. These suppliers can offer more personalized advice and ensure that the wood meets the necessary standards for your project.

While Japan is not known for an extensive renovation culture like countries such as Sweden or the United States, the interest in home improvement is steadily growing. As a result, new large-scale home centers are popping up across the country. Stores like KOHNAN PRO, Super Viva Home, and CAINZ HOME are some popular names where you can find a wide range of products for your projects.* I don't have a particular favorite, I just use whichever one is most convenient for the various errands I need to run that day, especially if I have rented a car or Kei Truck for the purpose.

If you don't want to rent a car for the whole day, the home centers offer a fantastic service—borrowing a truck for up to two hours to transport your purchased materials home immediately. This convenience has proven invaluable, allowing me to start working on my projects right away and saving precious time as I don't have to go rent a vehicle separately before going to the home center. Being able to drive the materials home instantly has been a game-changer for my projects.

For DIY enthusiasts like us, the thrill of scavenging through used marketplaces, vintage stores, online auctions, flea markets, and the Craigslist "free" listings for hidden treasures is unmatched. Granted, it can be a bit time-consuming, and you'll undoubtedly encounter your fair share of "lost in translation" moments at first when the

---

* As always, the links are in the "More Information" chapter!

Japanese translation function doesn't quite do the job. But you can keep your renovation costs at a minimum by using reclaimed and used materials so it's worth the time and effort.

And sometimes, you just have to work with what's in front of you, even if it means straying from your ideal design. If you ever find yourself struggling, start with the Facebook Groups. People there are incredibly helpful and willing to offer guidance and support. In the end, it's all about embracing the challenges and finding creative solutions along the way.

Japan's renovation culture might not be as extensive as in the US or Sweden, where DIY and home renovation are practically national pastimes. However, I firmly believe that a renovation "gold rush" is on the horizon in Japan. Old and affordable real estate is becoming increasingly popular, and the trend of renovating apartments and houses is catching on. Sure, there might be compromises to make when you can't find the exact materials you initially envisioned, but as renovation gains even more traction, these challenges will likely become easier to overcome.

🔑 12

Navigating Your Renovation

Looking back at it, despite not knowing much about the market, buying the Tree House in Tokyo was relatively easy. I never could have imagined how hard it was to renovate, find good contractors for electricity work, or to get rid of trash in Tokyo. Most of my friends here in Japan work within the modeling and entertainment industry, and they were little-to-no help at all.

Except for Canadian Senpai, who has been an invaluable resource to me since I met him that day in Shibuya. Thank you for all your advice my friend! I don't know where in the world I would have been or what I would have done without you!

Among my friends in Japan who have taken the akiya route, including Canadian Senpai and myself, there's a common thread—we all share a knack for DIY and woodworking. I'm not talking about being an engineer or an architect, but rather finding joy in creating with our hands. It could be reviving worn-out paint, laying new floors, or even transforming salvaged wood into something beautiful. Even the satisfaction of putting together IKEA furniture solo is part of the thrill. There's URLs for short videos of two of my finished houses and one of Ito-san's in progress houses in the "More Information" chapter.

Unlike countries like Sweden or the US, where renovation cultures are robust, Japan doesn't really have a DIY culture. With a penchant for new construction and a preference for professionals over self-renovation, renovating abandoned houses hasn't been a prominent trend in Japan. The term "akiya" doesn't spark interest and enthusiasm for most locals. However, a recent surge in the renovation sector involves companies acquiring aging apartments and sprucing them up. The renovated apartment is called a rifo mu manshon (リフォ無 マンション). Yet, for the ultimate buyer, customizing materials is limited due to the renovation company's prior choices. So, the options are either purchasing an old apartment and seeking a makeover service or embracing the do-it-yourself spirit—like my friends and I do.

Opting to renovate an old house or apartment on your own is time-consuming and potentially costly. If you've got the money, hiring help is a good option. If time is your ally, you might tackle the work yourself. And if you lack expertise, learning is the way to go.

Of course, certain tasks like electrical work, plumbing, and structural changes are best left to professionals. Seeking their guidance before you start is essential. But there are plenty of tasks you can handle. Who doesn't enjoy turning something worn into something wonderful?

Here's the catch: Japan lacks a widespread renovation culture. People aren't generally skilled in simple woodworking or fixing common issues like peeling wallpaper or unpleasant bathroom odors. When I reach out to unfamiliar companies, I often get surprisingly high price quotes. Need to connect a hose to your washing machine? ¥72,500 ($500). Installing a new blender in the kitchen? ¥145,000 ($1,000), *not including the blender*. It's astonishing.

A recent incident illustrates this dynamic. I connected some friends who specialize in renovation with an elderly woman in Shinjuku. She's in her 70s, living in an 80s-era house. Facing toilet troubles, she needed a replacement. Her son, a stylist, sought my advice and I introduced them.

I knew my renovation friends could help her. My friends have a unique approach—they acquire nearly new air conditioners and toilets from houses about to be demolished. During COVID they got about fifty top-notch TOTO toilets from bankrupt hotels and ryokans (旅館)—traditional Japanese inns—for free due to Japan's aversion to waste. Valued at ¥290,000–¥435,000 ($2,000–$3,000) each, these toilets come with remote controls, bidets, and heated seats. Two of these toilets ended up in my Sangenjaya House, and my friends installed one of them in the stylist's mum's house. Everyone was happy.

But here's where it gets interesting. The stylist's mum was happy with her new toilet, but she started to smell something bad. My advice? Contact my renovation friends—it's probably a simple fix and they can fix it. Instead, she hired another company that convinced her the job was botched and sold her a brand-new toilet for ¥435,000 ($3,000). On top of that, they charged her ¥43,500 ($300) for getting rid of the perfectly good TOTO toilet.

This story puzzles me. A minor issue that could likely be fixed, but the allure of *New* is so strong, that the stylist's mum believed this story about needing a *New* toilet. Shifting this perspective is a challenge. When I was learning Japanese, I came across the term mottainai (もったいない) early on. It means "what a waste" and is often used by Japanese people. Mottainai!

———————————— 🔑 ————————————

Mottainai! What a waste!

WHAT I WISH I HAD KNOWN

If I had to start my journey over from the beginning again, there are a lot of things I would have done differently, or wish I could have done differently. First off, I wish I hadn't stressed so much. Secondly, I wish I had asked more questions. And, finally, I wish I had spoken Japanese better at the time!

Let me share a few things from my learnings that will make your renovation journey easier from the start.

Community

Build a community from day one. Talk to your neighbors, knock on their door with a small omiyage (お土産), a gift. Say "yoroshiku onegai shimasu" (よろしくお願いします). Get to know the kinjo kaichō (

近所会長), the neighborhood president. Contribute to your community and they will have your back, and you will have theirs. Community and getting along with your neighbors is everything. You've heard all the stories about how all of my friends and neighbors have helped me in various ways. The Lumber Guy has saved me many times, introducing me to skilled professionals, teaching me where to throw trash, letting me pay my invoices months later. People from your community will help you!

Be Resourceful

Japan is a unique and amazing place, and as we've been discussing this entire book, things don't always work here the way you may be used to them working, wherever you are from. Being resourceful and creative is going to serve you well in everything you do here.

One of the most exciting moments during my DIY renovation of the Tree House was the creation of the staircase. Picture this: I had just given away the old, rickety brown aluminum ladder that led to the loft. Now, how would I access the second floor? A new ladder wasn't exactly the proper solution, especially when it comes to midnight trips to the bathroom.

I decided to build a staircase. Not just any staircase, but one with storage space beneath it. It was all about making the most of the space while ensuring it looked good. But the Tree House had a quirky layout with slanted walls and structural beams scattered around, which made constructing the staircase a real puzzle. Nevertheless, I was determined because, let's be honest, who wants a ladder when you can have a staircase?

I crunched numbers and made sketches, all while nervously examining the structural challenges. The staircase needed to reach about 2.3 m (~7.5 ft) in height and include a right-hand turn. To prepare, I spent evenings crafting miniature models from cardboard and glue. Finally, I decided to take the plunge and tackle this project solo.

There was just one hitch—I hadn't yet figured out where to source the right materials. In the end, I settled for the most budget-friendly 12 mm (0.472 in) thick plywood for the entire structure. The final landing, where you'd step off the staircase, featured a lighter flooring material to match the loft floor. It was probably the most cost-effective option available.

Japanese plywood comes in standard sheets measuring 91 x 182 cm (~36 in x 72 in), or three shaku x six shaku (remember our discussion of Japanese measurements?). To make my design work, I had to make numerous cuts and glue several pieces together. This was before I knew about the places to find quality wood and that home centers could cut it to size for a small fee. Looking back, I realize I could have done things more efficiently, but at the time this was the approach that made the most sense to me.

I spent a significant amount of time carefully calculating angles, diligently sawing steps with an old, inexpensive saw, and securing brackets to the wall for added support. Underneath the final landing, right beneath the loft, I inserted two 1-meter-long (3.28 feet) pieces of 2x4 wood to enhance stability.The process of building this staircase was not just rewarding; it was a lot of fun. It's incredibly sturdy and beautiful, so much so that even prominent Japanese interior magazines have sent their photographers to take pictures of it.

In the grand scheme of things, I spent less than ¥14,500 ($100) on materials and completed the entire project in less than a weekend. However, the real time investment was in the weeks of contemplation and the courage it took to bring this vision to life. I take pride in my budget-friendly plywood staircase, proof that DIY renovations can be both practical and stylish.

Trust Yourself

Trusting your community is crucial, as we've discussed, but sometimes you also have to trust your gut. At one point, Canadian Senpai gave me the leftovers from a treasure of small tiles he bought cheap online—around 50 m² (538 ft²) of small tiles I could play and learn with. I used these for various projects in my houses—bathroom tiles and backsplashes. But when it came to the kitchen in Sangenjaya House, I knew I wanted something really special, really striking.

I stumbled upon a local ramen restaurant in Sangenjaya, which had floor-to-ceiling tiles on the walls. I knew that was what I wanted to do, but what color? The ramen place had light green tiles which were really pretty, but the rest of the main floor of Sangenjaya house had a distinctly Scandinavian vibe with natural colors. For weeks, I wrestled with the decision—should I go bold with the lively green or opt for something more subdued?

In the end, I chose classic white subway tiles. Looking back, it was the right choice. They perfectly complement the wood and have a timeless elegance that colorful tiles might not have maintained.

From a DIY perspective, the job was challenging and pushed my tiling skills to the limit. The kitchen at Sangenjaya House has two windows over the countertop. Any DIY-tile-project survivors in the room? With spaces like that, it's always challenging to figure out where to line up the tile so it looks seamless and doesn't leave a weird gap or teeny-tiny slice of tile at any of the borders.

Once we figured that out, it was a total team effort. My girl-friend, my friends, and me, tirelessly working for three long days. On the third night, we worked until 4 am, finishing up by applying the final gray grout. We celebrated our success with champagne. Naturally.

That night, I slept soundly, proud of the tile work we had accomplished—possibly my best to date.

As a side note, modern Japanese kitchens often lean towards panels for their cost-effectiveness and ease of cleaning. While requiring a bit more effort, tiles can infuse sophistication and character that panels lack. So, if you're feeling adventurous, consider adding some tiles to your DIY toolkit—they might just become your new creative outlet.

WORKING WITH CONTRACTORS

Not everything you want to do in your project can be done by you. As we talked about in Chapter 10, "Planning Your Renovation," you can't do your own electrical work in Japan, and you probably don't want to do your own plumbing or structural projects. One way or the other, you are going to need help.

But there are some challenges here. There is a shortage of workers in the Japanese construction industry. According to a survey conducted by the Japan Federation of Construction Contractors, the construction industry is grappling with a significant shortage of skilled carpenters. The survey was part of the "General Employment Placement Status" report announced by the Ministry of Health, Labor and Welfare in January 2022, and it reveals alarming statistics on the severity of the issue.

A ratio of how many open job postings for a particular job is a crucial indicator of labor demand and supply, called the active job opening ratio, was reported as follows for various construction-related occupations:

- **Construction/mining occupation:** 4.86 times
- **Construction frame work occupation:** 8.56 times
- **Construction occupation:** 3.95 times
- **Electric work occupation:** 3.23 times
- **Civil engineering occupation:** 5.70 times
- **Mining occupation:** 4.98 times

These figures highlight the current nature of the industry, making it increasingly difficult to attract and secure skilled carpenters.

The shortage of carpenters can be attributed to a combination of factors, as revealed by the survey:

- **Chronic Long Working Hours:** The survey indicates that a substantial portion of construction sites (70%) struggle to provide even one proper day off per week, primarily due to the need to meet construction schedules.
- **Inadequate Wages:** Despite the perception of carpentry as a potentially high-income profession, the survey suggests that the prevalence of overtime work and self-financed expenses can lead to relatively lower earnings when calculated on a per-hour or per-day basis.

- **Precarious Employment:** Carpenters often work on a project basis, which can result in inconsistent income due to factors such as weather and the number of active sites. The lack of stability compared to full-time positions contributes to a higher attrition rate.

- **Work Hazards:** The survey underscores the inherent risks of construction work, emphasizing the concerns regarding injuries and accidents that further dissuade potential carpenters from joining the industry.

- **Aging Workforce and Lack of Young Entrants:** The construction industry's aging workforce, with nearly 30% of workers over the age of 55, coupled with a dearth of young individuals entering the field, threatens the continuity of skilled carpentry.

I've had many good experiences working with contractors, but I've also had my share of challenges.

I vividly recall the day I received the keys to my Sangenjaya House, granting me access to explore every nook of the house and the quaint garden in the back. At that time, an idea popped into my head—why not build a sauna in this small space? After all, I was embracing Scandinavian living in Japan, a country currently experiencing a sauna craze. Much like my decision regarding the tiles, I'm delighted I didn't go through with it. By putting a sauna in this space I would have blocked sunlight from that big southwest facing glass door, making the first floor substantially darker. Plus, to be honest, it probably would have turned into a storage unit after a few years like all of my friend's saunas in Sweden.

Instead I transformed the space into a little oasis. It's now a Japanese rotenburo (露天風呂), an outdoor space. It has a Japa-

nese-style soaking tub—ofuro (お風呂)—that I told you about in the last chapter. Complete with a charming shower and hinoki (檜) planks (Japanese cypress planks) covering the gray concrete block wall, the whole space has a rustic, luxurious feel that perfectly complements the aesthetic of the house.

Unfortunately, I had already poured the concrete slab under the house before tackling this outdoor space, which meant I had to purchase sand, gravel, and cement and mix them by hand in the sweltering Tokyo summer heat. Fortunately, my friends Paris, Kevin, Lia, and Yoshiko lent their helping hands, and we dedicated a full day to this endeavor, including a trip to the local home center, which even provided us with a truck to haul the one ton of materials. This concrete foundation makes the garden easy to maintain and keeps termites at bay.

But here's the incident that underscores the significance of choosing the right professionals. I wanted to repurpose a remaining piece from a ceiling beam for this outdoor shower area. It seemed like a practical way to reduce waste and infuse character into the space. The plumber I hired didn't share my vision.

The good plumbers are always crazy busy, and none of my usual people were available. My friend Yuchan-san, a surfer friend who runs several izakayas (居酒屋) in Tokyo, introduced me to a new plumber. He was an older man, about 65 years old.

The plumber arrived on a summer day in Tokyo, and it was scorching hot, 40 °C (104 °F). He proceeded to strip naked and do the plumbing in his underwear. I admit I liked that attitude! Very European. But also really unprofessional.

Next he drilled big holes in the street with his jackhammer in order to connect the pipes. His plumber's license gives him the authority to do this, but it still requires getting permission from the municipality before you tear up the road. This guy hadn't gotten the permission and everyone was concerned. My neighbors came over and told me, "Anton, he can't do that!" Even my surfer friend said, "Anton, this is not okay!" (Fortunately, two weeks later the contractors who had to make holes in the street for the new gas line fixed the plumber's holes as well, as a favor to me, so I didn't have to call the municipality and beg for forgiveness.)

I knew things were not going well, but I still needed help with my outdoor shower. There were pipes on the outside wall of the house to supply water to the shower head, and I wanted to use the old beam that I'd reclaimed from the interior construction to cover them up. I explained to the plumber my vision, I wanted to carve a channel out of the back of this wooden beam to cover the pipes and make it look like it was part of the wall.

Despite my explanation, he proceeded to work on the project for two days without using the wood.

When I asked him about it, he said, "It's not possible. You can't have wood in a shower area. It's not doable."

I, again, explained the idea of carving a channel out of the back to make space for the pipes, to make it beautiful.

He said, "This is how I've done things for fifty years, I have never seen this, and I will not do this."

That was, unfortunately, the last straw. I could deal with plumbing in underwear, and I could make nice with the municipality about the road, but I couldn't live with ugly exposed pipes when there was such a great solution available.

When I broke the news that I had to let him go, he was very apologetic.

"Gomen (ごめん)," he said, over and over. (I'm sorry.)

"Warukatta ne (悪かったね)." (That was bad of me.)

I felt bad for him, so I helped him pack all of his things. He'd done about half the work on the job, so I paid him half the money, and then he left.

This incident served as a valuable lesson about the importance of effective communication and finding professionals who are willing to collaborate and align with your ideas.

My new plumber understood my vision and the final result exudes the serene ambiance of a Japanese onsen (温泉), a traditional outdoor bathing area or hot spring. The wooden bathtub, in particular, adds a touch of luxurious Japanese living to the entire house. The cypress covering on the block walls at the back, along with a sleek black shower head, with the pipes ingeniously hidden behind the reclaimed beam, add to the aesthetic. Of course, one of the best features is the abundant natural light that filters into the house.

Before I settled on the final vision for the outdoor space at Sangenjaya House, I considered creating a more conventional garden or even a traditional Japanese rock garden with stones and gravel, as my architect friend Christian suggested. While these options would have been simpler and more traditionally Japanese, I opted for something different, and the result turned out great!

Over my years of DIY endeavors, I've come to realize that those initial ideas we have when we first see a space often evolve into something far better as we spend more time there. The first hour you enter a room you plan to remodel, it feels like a blank canvas ready for dramatic changes. However, your final vision, when compared to your real, finished project, often turns out to be quite different.

Here's a fun experiment for your next renovation project: Record your initial thoughts and ideas in writing or on video the first time you enter the space. Don't revisit this footage until you've completed your project. I think you'll find the difference between your initial thoughts and your final result can be quite fascinating.

🔑 13

Removing Your Trash

Doing the demolition work on the Sangenjaya House created a lot of trash. If you've ever done demo on a renovation, you know what I mean. It seems to multiply in volume in a way that is hard to fully explain. I piled it on the tiny patio. I piled it in the center of the house. I piled it everywhere. Eventually the piles got so big I knew I had to deal with them. There wasn't any room to work anymore. The piles had to go.

Except there was a problem.

As I've told you, one of the reasons that I was able to buy Sangenjaya House for such a good price is because it is on a non-rebuildable property situated on a very narrow road, only 2 m (6.5 ft) wide. The street is so narrow that you can't fit a car on it at all. The nearest driveable road is at the intersection 30 m (~100 ft) away, and *that* road is only 3 m (9.8 ft) wide. It's so narrow that you can't legally park on it—no other car would be able to get around you. So the typical idea of renting a truck, backing it up to the house and spending the day loading it with all of the debris was completely out of the question. No access on the back either, no alley, no driveway, no garage. No access at all except in the teeny tiny street that I couldn't park on.

And also? Everything had to be meticulously sorted and bagged up correctly in order to be taken to the disposal facility. I was going to need a lot of bags, and I was going to need a truck small enough to fit on my tiny street.

Then I was going to need a little creativity, a little stress management, and a lot of hustle.

This is what I had to do:

1. Break down all the debris into pieces small enough to fit into bags.
2. Carry all the bags to the front of the house and pile them up where they were easily accessible (you'll see why in a second).
3. Bring a teeny-tiny pickup truck, called a kei truck, or keitora (軽トラ), down the teeny-tiny (but drivable) road at the end of my street.
4. Park illegally at the intersection.
5. Get out of the teeny-tiny pickup truck and run the 30 m (~100 ft) to my house to get as many bags as I could carry.
6. Run 30 m (~100 ft) back to the teeny-tiny pickup truck.
7. Rinse and repeat until someone was behind the truck and I had to move it.
8. Go around the block and do it again.
9. And again.
10. Again.
11. And then again, again.

Once the truck was filled, of course, I could drive it to the disposal station and pay for the privilege of dumping it, but back at the house, the whole process would start over again. I could usually only get one or two loads before someone would be in a car waiting, and I'd have to move the truck, going around the block again. Sometimes when I pulled onto my street again there'd already be someone right behind me, and I'd have to go around the block again and again.

Then it was back to moving bags.

Grab a couple of bags, move the truck.

Grab a bag, move the truck.

Go around the block.

Grab a bag, move the truck.

Even after working on it for ages, I didn't get it all by the time I had to return the truck. I couldn't quite fit in the last square meter (10.8 ft²) of debris. Fortunately it was burnables, so I've been chopping it up and putting it out with the other burnables that get picked up with the regular trash service.

As of this writing, there's still a little bit left, but choko choko (ちょこちょこ), little by little, the trash is going away. I can't express how relieved I'll feel after the last of the trash is finally gone. Like Christmas.

In my experience the hardest thing with renovating in Japan is getting rid of trash.

DISPOSING OF TRASH

Trash disposal in Japan is a challenge that often catches newcomers by surprise, and it's a facet of property renovation that should not be underestimated. You might be thinking, "How hard can it be to dispose of trash?" I hope my story has answered that question. It can be quite the ordeal, and that's not just because of narrow streets.

Considering how you'll deal with the trash will be as critical as your design and construction plans on your renovation project. It's not just about the financial aspect, although disposal costs can add up significantly. It's about navigating a system that involves precise sorting, adhering to strict schedules, and respecting the environment and community.

For instance, disposing of burnable waste entails cutting it into pieces no longer than 30 cm (~12 in) and following designated collection procedures. This might seem manageable for day-to-day waste, but when you're dealing with larger quantities, especially during a whole-house renovation, individually bagging and handling all the waste becomes challenging. In such cases, renting, or borrowing, a truck to transport the waste to the appropriate disposal site is often the more efficient choice.

Now, let's talk costs. Disposing of construction waste, for example, involves meticulous sorting, loading the waste onto the truck and transporting it to a private dump near Futago-Tamagawa (二子玉川). At the dump, they assess the load visually and charge you based on the cubic meter of waste. The cost varies depending on the type of waste, burnable waste being the cheapest, while materials like concrete, stone, and other landfill items can cost up to ¥29,000 ($200) per cubic meter (35.3 cubic feet). These expenses can add up quickly, and disposal fees are on the rise. Also, if you fail to sort your waste properly before arriving, you might be hit with an additional surcharge.

My first encounter with the costs of trash disposal was when I tackled the trash from my initial property, the Tree House. I vividly recall the moment when I reluctantly paid around ¥174,000

❢

WHY JAPANESE CITIES REMOVED THEIR TRASH CANS

When contemplating the cleanliness of Japan's urban landscape, the scarcity of public trash cans might make you curious: "How does Japan stay so immaculate with so few trash bins?" A great question, as the streets of Tokyo, despite their hustle and bustle, maintain a remarkable level of cleanliness.

The lack of public trash cans in Tokyo is a response to the 1995 Tokyo Subway attack by the cult Aum Shinrikyo. Removing the trash cans prioritizes safety by reducing potential hiding spots for dangerous items. This approach aligns with Japan's cultural values of personal responsibility and cleanliness, and is the reason your tuna-mayonnaise onigiri (お握り) wrapper suddenly becomes an unexpected back-pocket companion after a day of city exploration.

Japanese society places strong emphasis on conscientious waste management and adherence to stringent manners. As a result, many locals opt to carry their trash until an appropriate disposal site is found. While this practice reflects a collective commitment to cleanliness, it does present an inconvenience for those navigating the city with waste in tow.

($1,200) to have someone take care of my waste. Looking back, armed with the knowledge I've acquired since then, I believe I could have disposed of five times the amount for that same cost.

If you're in more rural areas, you'll find a somewhat different scenario. Many rural regions have efficient incinerators, and you're charged based on the weight you're offloading. But in the heart of central Tokyo, it's a bit more complicated, and can sometimes feel like an adventure in itself.

I totally get it—focusing on disposal costs might not be the most exciting part of your project. But here's the thing: while buying a plaster board could be cheap at around ¥500 (~$3.50) a sheet, the cost to dispose of it can be double that at ¥1000 ($7). Not the most fun fact to think about. But a reality you are going to have to deal with. So before you start shopping for your renovation, take a moment to plan how you'll handle getting rid of things later. It might not be the most glamorous aspect, but it's a smart move to avoid unexpected costs, and disposal challenges down the road. Planning for disposal is as crucial as planning for design and construction. Never forget this.

SODAI GOMI: JAPAN'S WAY OF HANDLING BIG TRASH

In Japan, taking out the big stuff—like old furniture and appliances—is a bit different. They have something called sodai gomi (粗大ごみ) which means oversized garbage. This way of handling big trash shows how Japan cares about keeping things clean and neat. It's all part of their commitment to taking care of the environment, even when getting rid of old stuff.

In my area, for example, we put out cans, bottles, and cardboard on Sundays. Food waste goes out on Tuesdays and Fridays. If you're moving and need to toss out big things, like beds or chairs, you need to plan ahead and pay a fee. When you have something large to get rid of, you contact your local municipality. You let them know what you want to throw away. They'll tell you how much it will cost and give you a date when they can come pick it up.

This can be a bit tricky. The pickup dates are usually quite far in advance—sometimes it takes three to four weeks before they can come. This can be a challenge, especially for people who are moving apartments and need to clear out big things quickly.

After you arrange the pickup date, you go to the convenience store to buy sodai gomi stickers with the correct value. Much like buying the right value of stamps when sending a postcard. The municipality will tell you how much the stickers need to be worth. You write your name and date on the stickers and put them on the items you're getting rid of. When the scheduled pickup day arrives, you place your items outside with the stickers on them, and the municipality takes them away.

While Japan's approach to sodai gomi helps keep the streets clean and organized, it can create some difficulties when you're in a rush or need to move. Planning ahead, buying the right stickers, and following the process is essential to ensure that you have enough time to properly dispose of your oversized items, especially when life changes are on the horizon. Or when you are about to renovate an old house you acquired.

THINGS LEFT BEHIND

When you buy an old house in Japan, sometimes, to make it easy for the seller, you buy the house as is. As I've said before, I never ask for a home inspection, and I've bought houses full of old belongings and things that needed to be sorted through and cleaned out. This is more common when you buy an akiya, especially if you buy a house direct from the owner that wasn't prepared to be on the market, like Sangenjaya House in Tokyo. If you watch my YouTube series *Tokyo Renovation Diaries*, you'll see that the previous owners left everything behind.*

If you watch that video, you may think it looks like a nightmare, or you might think it looks like fun. Everyone has a different reaction. I thought it was a little bit fun—but I like to hunt for treasure. It was also a little bit of a cultural study. There were old Japanese magazines, photographs, kimonos, newspapers, and a huge vinyl and CD-collection. Everything left behind.

I was able to send many of the clothes home to my mom and sisters, including a leather jacket that my sister's boyfriend is still wearing. There were a lot of kimonos, which my mom is using, giving them to guests and friends who come to visit. Interestingly, old kimonos have little value in Japan, but if you export them then they're worth twenty times more. There was a very cool, large, green kitchen scale from the

* The URL is in the "More Information" chapter!

🔑

MOTTAINAI

Earlier we talked about mottainai (もったいない). The word mottainai is a Japanese word that has been adopted by environmentalists world-wide. Roughly meaning, "what a waste!" it expresses regret for wasting things and is used to encourage people to reduce, reuse, and recycle. A well-known environmentalist named Wangari Maathai used the word mottainai at the United Nations to inspire people to protect the environment.

In Japan, people appreciate vintage clothes, showing how valuable things from the past can be. But, in contrast, the Japanese often throw away big things like houses and appliances when they get old, instead of reusing, recycling, or renovating them. This shows a gap between our appreciation for old things and how we treat important items in our society. It's my opinion that we should aim to apply the mottainai idea to everything, not just fashion, and be more mindful of our resources. Unlike in Europe or America where the phrase "Save This House" is commonly used to advocate for preserving old houses, I've never heard this kind of sentiment expressed in Japan.

Isn't it weird to not maintain a house, or renovate an old home? And that in many cases they will tear down an old house to build something brand new? Mottainai!

50s or 60s that can measure up to three kilos (6.6 pounds). I took that to Sweden to give to my mom. It still proudly stands in the kitchen window, very beautiful.

Then there was the six-hundred-plus vinyl collection—amazing. I gave the whole lot to a friend who runs a vinyl bar called Quintet. He still has all of them and is hoping to find a way to archive them somehow. Meanwhile, if you come to Tokyo to visit, you can visit my friend at Quintet and hear some of the records for yourself. I've put the address of his place in the "More Information" chapter so you can find him when you come here.

One thing I am particularly proud of saving from the house are the pair of wooden kimono chests, tansu (タンス), that were left by the previous owner. The big old chests are made of paulownia wood, kiri (桐), and sit majestically in one of the bedrooms in the Sangenjaya House, exactly where they have been for decades.

Much like my Sangenjaya House, many houses in Japan come with this unusual bonus—belongings left behind

by previous owners. The responsibility for clearing out this (potential) treasure trove typically falls on the new buyer, and this arrangement can actually make the property more enticing to some sellers. I won't sugarcoat it; dealing with this unexpected treasure can be a fair amount of work. However, the upside is that you can often secure these houses at a substantial discount.

My friend, Isozaki-san, who specializes in investing in abandoned houses, once acquired a property for roughly ¥870,000 ($6,000), and it took him a week of dedicated cleaning to empty the place. Imagine his surprise when, amid the piles of discarded items, he stumbled upon a collection of old stamps. He later sold this unexpected find for over ¥2.9 million ($20,000)! Isozaki-san frequently reminds me that when the previous owner was a teacher or a dedicated collector, there's a high likelihood they've left behind valuables. These treasures, hidden amidst the clutter, might go unnoticed by the inheritor, who often underestimates their value. So, when you're considering a property purchase in Japan, don't be too quick to dismiss the idea of inheriting someone else's trash. It could very well contain hidden gems that, with some effort, could turn your investment into a real treasure.

Getting rid of all of the left-behind things in Sangenjaya House turned out to be an adventure as well. Some of the things were beautiful and interesting, but there was a lot of trash, too, and I needed to clear it out before I could start renovating. In Setagaya-ku (世田谷区), where Sangenjaya House is, the municipality told me I could dispose of my trash, so I signed up for a pick-up date. I had to wait two months, and when they finally came, they said I could only throw away twelve items. Twelve items! I couldn't help but laugh. But it wasn't really funny. I couldn't start renovating until all the old stuff was gone.

I started searching online and got quotes from sketchy companies who rudely pointed out how old and messy my house was—as if I didn't know that already! The highest quote I received was a whopping ¥2,175,000 ($15,000) to haul away my trash. It was a sum I neither had nor wanted to spend. Luckily, my friend Paris introduced me to a friend of his who runs a company in Kanagawa (神奈川県) called Forever.

Forever does cleaning and trash disposal. They come to your location and take care of *everything*. They have a big warehouse in Kanagawa where they bring everything from your home and take care of, sort, recycle, sell, and deal with it. ***All of it***. They don't have their own store but will sell many of the things they find to retailers if they understand it has value. It's incredibly helpful, and worth it for many people (including me). Even if the owner of an akiya (or a regular home that's overly full) understands their belongings hold value they sometimes don't have time or energy to deal with selling it and are relieved to just leave everything to a company like Forever.*

They came over, meticulously sorted through the things that had been left behind, and hauled it all away. A couple of weeks and ¥290,000 ($2,000) later, my house was finally clean.

ONE MORE BAG (STORY) OF TRASH

I get comments on my social media every time I post a trash related renovation video. Why don't you bury the dirt in your garden? Why don't you burn the trash? Why don't you dump it at another abandoned house in your area?

It seems so simple, but in reality none of these ideas would work. In Tokyo, land space is limited, and my garden is only six square meters 6 m² (64.6 ft²). Even if I wanted to bury dirt or trash (I don't), there's not enough room. Fires can pose a serious hazard in densely

---

* Find their contact information in the "More Information" chapter at the end of the book.

populated areas like Tokyo, so there's no way I'm burning the trash. Remember Chapter 1? Fires have devastated Japan many times. I'd like to not be the reason it happens again. And dumping my trash on another property is out of the question. I spend all of my time trying to make my neighborhood better by renovating and reviving houses. Why would I dump my trash on someone else's doorstep, even if it is an abandoned one? No. Just no.

When dealing with trash (like everything else in Japan), the best course of action is to follow the rules and be respectful. Show respect for the environment and community by using proper waste disposal methods.

When I renovated Liton House, before I renovated Sangenjaya House, I hadn't done a big demo project before, so I didn't realize just how fast those piles were going to pile up. I hadn't dealt with that amount of trash before, and I didn't (yet) know how hard it was going to be. Liton House has a small garden, about 7 m² (75 ft²), and at first this seemed like a convenient space to offload unwanted items and construction debris. For a few weeks, that's precisely what I did.

As the weeks passed, and the renovation progressed, and the pile got bigger and bigger, I knew it had to go. It was blocking my path, both literally and figuratively. I couldn't continue the demolition of the house with this growing mountain of debris in my way.

I did some calling around and found out that if I cut the pieces of wood into 30 cm (12 in) lengths or smaller, I could classify them as burnable trash. In Tokyo, we have dedicated burnable trash days on Tuesdays and Fridays each week, so this seemed like a viable solution. Armed with a rusty circular saw, I embarked on the arduous task of cutting the wood into manageable pieces. Surrounded by a chaotic jumble of discarded materials, it was far from an enjoyable job. Worse yet, it was a bit dangerous; a wrong move with the saw or hitting an old screw buried in the wood could cause the saw to jump or buck—potentially very dangerous.

I worked and worked, cutting and bagging, cutting and bagging. Despite my hard work and dedication, the pile of trash seemed to grow, not shrink. I reached a point where I had to resort to buying plastic bags and packing the wood into them, just to make some headway.

Finally, I realized I was going to have to get some help. I needed to free up space in order to continue the renovation. This was during the peak of the COVID pandemic in Japan, a time when people were wary of close contact and mask-wearing was the norm. But I was desperate and a friend of a friend offered assistance.

They came to visit my house, all of us masked up and cautious, making sure to keep our distance from each other. My friend had brought along an acquaintance who ran a construction company. Despite the restrictions and the challenges, they offered to come back the next day at 7 am to take away all the remaining trash for a fee of about ¥116,000 ($800). Trash problem solved. Thank goodness,

As I shared at the start of the chapter, when I renovated Sangenjaya House in the same neighborhood, I borrowed a kei truck and was able to do the disposal myself. But that first time, with COVID happening, borrowing a truck just wasn't an option. I'm so grateful I had extended community to help me, otherwise I would have been stuck with a half-finished renovation until COVID was over.

THE LAST (?) WORD ON TRASH

My advice is this: do not underestimate trash disposal in Japan. I'm sharing this insight so that you don't find yourself buried in a pile of trash bags down the road. Well, more accurately, you'll have a plan *for when* you find yourself buried in a pile of trash bags. Because, let's be honest, it's a renovation. The pile of trash bags is going to happen. It's just a matter of how you're going to deal with them so they don't stop you from getting your renovation done.

Before buying an old house ask yourself: do you know how to get rid of this? Before buying building materials or bulky furniture, ask yourself: do you know how to get rid of these things when you're done with them? There are questions that can save you both headaches and expenses.

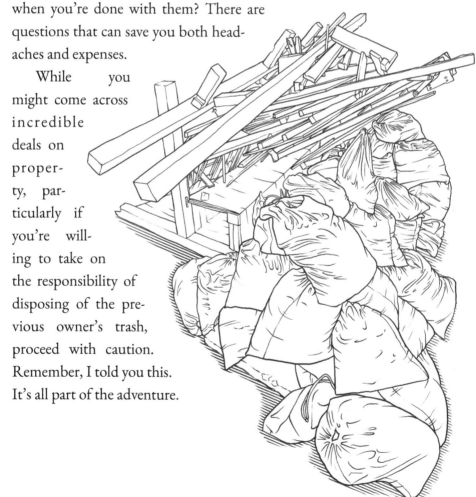

While you might come across incredible deals on property, particularly if you're willing to take on the responsibility of disposing of the previous owner's trash, proceed with caution. Remember, I told you this. It's all part of the adventure.

Part 4
MONETIZING

🔑 14

Operating an Airbnb

You've decided that you're going to purchase a property and renovate it. Great, now how are you going to make money from that property? We discussed different ways to monetize your property in Chapter 4, "Exploring Investment Opportunities." One way to make money (and one that I personally enjoy) is by running it as an Airbnb.

But here's the truth: running an Airbnb isn't a walk in the park; it's a labor of love. It involves more than just sitting back and watching the money roll in. There are licenses to secure, guests and neighbors to keep content, meticulous cleaning and maintenance to uphold to ensure the property remains in top-notch condition. However, if you genuinely enjoy the hospitality business, like I do, and you're willing to put in the effort, the rewards can be extraordinary.

UNLOCKING AIRBNB SUCCESS

You've taken the plunge and invested in a house in Japan, with the brilliant idea of transforming it into a lucrative Airbnb short-term rental. Whether your property is freshly renovated or you're about to start the renovation adventure, you're on the right track. Let's start by reviewing a set of steps to succeeding in the world of Airbnb hosting and earn a great return.

Step 1: Know Your Market

Like any savvy businessperson, research is your trusty sidekick. Start by understanding the demand in your area. Are couples, families, or solo travelers frequenting your locale? Dive deep into market trends, and don't hesitate to take inspiration from stunning listings that catch your eye. What other Airbnb's are near your property and how are they priced? What are the amenities they offer? What stands out about them? What catches your eye about their decor, gardens, or vibe? What's unique? What's expected? How will your place offer the things people want but also have things that are different, unusual or unexpected? Familiarize yourself with your potential guests, their preferences, and what makes them click that magical "BOOK NOW" button.

Step 2: Create a Unique Haven

The key to Airbnb success? Making your space stand out. When it comes to furnishing, I have a little secret—I buy used furniture. Why? Because it infuses my places with character and uniqueness. And that's precisely what you need to entice potential guests. Identify what's missing in your area and build your furnishing strategy from there. Remember, pictures are everything. Take them in the soft, inviting light of day. A big shoutout to David Lundin, whose stellar photos of my Sangenjaya House has led to us being fully booked since our listing went live.

Step 3: Craft Your Unique Selling Point (USP)

Speaking of standing out, let's take Sangenjaya House as an example—a Scandinavian-inspired Japanese dwelling nestled in a trendy Tokyo neighborhood. It's designed to cater to foreign families and groups seeking an authentic Japanese experience with a dash of modern comfort. Unlike the somewhat predictable, new 2x4 construction houses around, it exudes character and allure. Spacious, bathed in sunlight, and boasting a blend of modern amenities and traditional Japanese charm, it's unlike anything else in the area.

If you haven't already seen it, you should check out Caleb Simpson's video tour of Sangenjaya House (the link is in the "More Information" chapter). Caleb is an apartment tour guy from New York. He explored the house, left his signature in my guest book, and even spent the night there just before my hotel license was obtained. Sangenjaya House had been neglected for many years before I renovated it, and it's my flagship project. It was a real honor to have Caleb visit and show off how beautiful the house is. Thank you Caleb for being great!

Step 4: Price It Right

Yes, some might say my rates are on the higher side, starting at ¥60,000 (~$410) per night. But guests, especially families, are willing to pay a premium for spacious, comfortable accommodations. When you're offering an experience as unique as Sangenjaya House, you're in a league of your own. During peak holiday seasons, we charge double rates—because that's what the market demands. Don't shy away from setting your price based on your property's value.

Step 5: Service with a Smile

It's not just about the space; it's about the experience. I have a fantastic crew of cleaners who ensure our place sparkles before every guest arrives. There is always fresh greenery in the house as well. Don't underestimate the power of happy plants! Special occasions, like a honeymoon, get a little extra touch—like flowers and chocolate. I live nearby and love to personally welcome my guests. Sharing the house I've created and introducing them to Tokyo brings me immense joy.

The world of Airbnb hosting is a journey filled with unique experiences and personal connections that make the effort worthwhile. If you're ready to embark on this adventure in Japan, rest assured, the path to Airbnb success is within your grasp.

OBTAINING YOUR AIRBNB LICENSE IN JAPAN

In 2018, the Japanese government implemented new regulations to govern short-term vacation rentals, including those listed on platforms like Airbnb. These changes were aimed at striking a balance between promoting tourism and preserving residential communities. The impact was significant, and signs warning against illegal short-term rentals can still be found in many apartment buildings across Tokyo.

民泊禁止

MINPAKU KINSHI

SHORT TERM RENTALS FORBIDDEN

Before 2018, the Airbnb market in Japan was unregulated, and many people rented apartments and houses in their names to operate them as Airbnb rentals, making extra income. Canadian Senpai calls this time period the "Golden Years" of Airbnb. But by 2015 the market had become saturated, and in 2018 the government cracked down on illegal rentals, requiring all hosts to obtain licenses and comply with the new rules. Most listings disappeared from the platform almost overnight.

The COVID pandemic further impacted the Airbnb market, causing even more rentals to disappear as Japan closed its borders for almost three years. Post-COVID, with the borders reopened, tourists are now flocking back to the country, creating a surge in demand for accommodations. If you possess a well-located property in a great area, your Airbnb listing has the potential to be in high demand and consistently booked. With the right strategy, attention to the new regulations, and a welcoming property, you can tap into the growing tourism market and make your Airbnb venture a resounding success in Japan.

The process of getting an Airbnb license in Japan is complicated, and to get my hotel license for Sangenjaya House took months, with visits from local authorities and the fire brigade to check that everything was safe and proper. I also had to spend thousands of

🔑

MANSHON AIRBNB'S
ARE NEARLY IMPOSSIBLE

Before the Airbnb regulations changed in 2018, some people used to rent manshon apartments and then sublet them on Airbnb. This practice is nearly impossible now. Today, to get a hotel license for a manshon apartment you must obtain permission from the management company or landlord *plus* every other apartment owner in the building. This is basically impossible.

The one situation where it is somewhat possible is if the manshon building has a single owner; all of the apartments in the building are owned and managed by one person or company. In this case, it is possible to get permission and operate an Airbnb in the building, but such opportunities are rare and tend to involve older properties. There are cases where individuals have managed to operate Airbnb businesses in such buildings. I've contemplated pursuing this avenue myself—renting a spacious, older apartment in a prime location, customizing it to create a unique space, and then offering it on Airbnb. However, these properties quickly disappear from the market. Japanese real estate companies compete for similar spaces, transforming them into share-houses, office space, or Airbnb rentals themselves.

While it's not entirely impossible to execute this approach, I've come to the conclusion that it's not worth the effort. Let's consider the scenario of signing a two-year lease, investing time and resources to secure a hotel license, and finally starting Airbnb rentals four months later. What if the building owner witnesses the success of your venture? What if, when your lease is up, they decide to terminate your lease and take over the thriving business you painstakingly established? In such a situation, you'd be faced with the daunting task of relocating, disposing of furniture—potentially at a cost— and forfeiting your initial deposit. Meanwhile, the owner continues to profit from the business you initiated.

Buying a free-standing property is more appealing, as it circumvents these potential pitfalls. While the journey to owning a property might be more intricate, it provides a more stable foundation for pursuing Airbnb ventures without the shadow of uncertainty hanging overhead.

dollars to add emergency exit signs, emergency lights, class-A smoke alarms, and security cameras. All required in order to get the license.

I hired a friend of mine with expertise in getting an Airbnb license to get all of this done for me. If I hadn't hired my friend, I could have made a costly mistake, or delayed the process by additional months, resulting in lost income. Throughout the journey, I made sure to be actively involved and present during all the preparations, meetings, and appointments with officials. I saw this as a valuable learning opportunity, and I wanted to understand thoroughly how the process works. While it was challenging, the knowledge I gained and the success of obtaining the license made it all worthwhile.

Licenses for Airbnb in Japan

In Japan, a minpaku (民泊) license and a hotel license are two different types of permits required for operating lodging facilities, such as vacation rentals or accommodations for tourists. Keep in mind each area of Japan has different rules and regulations, and the regulations can vary, especially within the city center of Tokyo and tourist areas.

Minpaku License

Also known as a Private Lodging Business License, a minpaku license is required for individuals or businesses that provide lodging services in private homes or residential properties for a short-term period, typically for less than 180 days a year. Minpaku accommodations are often offered through platforms like Airbnb and other vacation rental websites.

A minpaku license allows property owners to legally rent out their homes or rooms to tourists and visitors for short stays. There are specific regulations and requirements for obtaining a minpaku license, including safety standards, property size limitations, and other local government regulations.

Hotel License

A hotel license is required for businesses operating commercial accommodations that provide lodging services for paying guests, and it covers a wide range of lodging facilities, including hotels, inns, guesthouses, and ryokans (旅館), traditional Japanese inns. Hotels are typically larger establishments with multiple rooms and additional facilities and services, such as restaurants, conference rooms, and other amenities. A hotel license allows you to rent out your property every day of the year, rather than the 180-day restriction of a minpaku license.

Obtaining a hotel license involves meeting more stringent requirements, such as building safety standards, health regulations, fire safety measures, and more comprehensive inspections by local authorities. Hotels are also subject to various national and local regulations, and the licensing process can be more complex and time-consuming compared to obtaining a minpaku license.

If you are considering operating a lodging facility in Japan and have the option to choose between a minpaku license and a hotel license, I would highly recommend going for a hotel license right from the start. While both licenses have their merits, there are certain advantages to obtaining a hotel license that can make it a more attractive choice for most property owners.

One of the main benefits of having a hotel license is that it allows you to utilize your rental property every day of the year without any restrictions on the number of days you can rent it out. With a minpaku license, there are limitations on the number of days you can rent out your property, usually capped at 180 days per year in many areas. This can be a significant limitation, especially if you want to maximize your rental income and cater to guests year-round.

Additionally, the licensing process for both minpaku and hotel licenses can be time-consuming and involve various regulatory requirements and inspections by local authorities. If you start with a minpaku license and later decide to switch to a hotel license, you will have to go through the entire licensing process again from scratch, which can be cumbersome and time-consuming. It is often more efficient and practical to aim for a hotel license from the beginning if your property and business plans meet the necessary criteria.

CONSIDERATION FOR YOUR NEIGHBORS

Obtaining a hotel license for your property opens up exciting opportunities, but it's essential to keep in mind that your venture won't just affect your guests. Your neighbors will also play a significant role in your hosting experience. Especially in my case, where my neighbors are elderly individuals who have witnessed my dedication firsthand. They've seen me tirelessly work day and night, braving Tokyo's scorching summers, cold winters, and rare snow, all while gradually transforming my house into something beautiful.

Through the journey, a heartwarming camaraderie has developed. These kind-hearted neighbors, who don't speak English at all, occasionally surprise me with thoughtful gifts, and in turn, I express my gratitude with tokens of appreciation. We've established a wonderful tradition of exchanging Christmas presents, and I've taken it upon myself to assist them in various ways despite the language barrier. From managing their trash to sharing leftover wood from my projects, I've made an effort to be a reliable and supportive presence.

My interactions with my non-English speaking neighbors highlight the universal language of care and kindness. Despite our linguistic differences, our shared sense of community transcends words. Their support and understanding have been instrumental in making my Airbnb venture successful. Without their encouragement, collaboration, and shared sense of care, utilizing my property for hosting wouldn't have been possible.

Be nice to people. Kindness and hard work transcends borders. Worship and treat your neighbors well. One angry neighbor can destroy your entire business. And besides, making friends and helping each other out is a much more fun approach in life.

AIRBNB TIPS

From my years of experience in hosting Airbnb rentals I've learned a lot. Here's some tips to successfully guide you in your Airbnb rental.

Property Eligibility

Not all properties are eligible for the Airbnb license. Certain areas, such as residential zones, might have restrictions on vacation rentals to maintain a peaceful living environment for local residents. Please check this before you buy your house, if your end-goal is to do Airbnb.

Research Thoroughly

Before diving into hosting, or even buying a place solely for the purpose of doing Airbnb, take the time to research and understand the rules and regulations related to short-term vacation rentals in this particular area. Familiarize yourself with the requirements for obtaining a license and the responsibilities that come with hosting guests.

Registration Number

After obtaining the license, hosts receive a registration number that must be displayed on their Airbnb listing. You can not create a listing without this number.

Safety Regulations

Hosts must comply with safety regulations, such as installing smoke detectors and fire extinguishers, to ensure the safety of guests.

Taxes

Airbnb hosts are subject to certain taxes, including consumption tax and accommodation tax. It is essential to understand and fulfill tax obligations related to your short-term rental income.

Communication with Neighbors

As I mentioned above, building a good relationship with neighbors is crucial. I recommend you inform them of your intention to operate an Airbnb and address any concerns they may have.

Language Barrier

Most official documents and processes may be in Japanese. Engaging a bilingual agent or seeking assistance from a property management company can help overcome language barriers.

Ongoing Monitoring

Local authorities may conduct periodic inspections to ensure hosts are complying with regulations. It's essential to stay up-to-date with any changes in the law or requirements.

Property Management Services

If managing an Airbnb property seems overwhelming, hiring a property management service can help handle day-to-day operations, guest communications, and legal compliance.

Be Well-Prepared

Obtaining a license and setting up your Airbnb property can be a time-consuming and intricate process. Be patient and make sure you have all the necessary documents and safety measures in place. This includes emergency exit signs, lights, smoke alarms, and other safety essentials.

Work With an Expert

The bureaucratic process of obtaining a license and setting up your Airbnb can be overwhelming, especially for foreigners. Consider working with a reputable middle-man or a knowledgeable expert who can guide you through the paperwork and liaise with the authorities on your behalf.

Create a Comfortable Space

Pay attention to the details of your Airbnb property to ensure your guests have a comfortable and enjoyable stay. Offer amenities that cater to their needs and make their experience memorable.

Embrace Cultural Exchange

Hosting on Airbnb offers a unique opportunity for cultural exchange with guests from around the world. Embrace this aspect, share your passion for Japan, and provide them with insights into local customs and traditions. What can you share with them?

Communicate Effectively

Clear and prompt communication with your guests is crucial for a smooth hosting experience. Be responsive to inquiries and provide them with useful information about the area and your property.

Build Positive Reviews

Positive reviews from previous guests can significantly impact your Airbnb's success. Strive to deliver exceptional hospitality and create a welcoming atmosphere to encourage favorable feedback.

Be Flexible and Adaptable

As the Airbnb landscape evolves, be open to adjusting your hosting strategy. Stay informed about market trends and guest preferences, and be willing to adapt your approach to meet changing demands.

Enjoy the Journey

Hosting on Airbnb is not just a business; it's an opportunity to connect with people from diverse backgrounds and share your love for Japan. Enjoy the journey, learn from each hosting experience, and cherish the memories you create with your guests.

MY EXPERIENCE AS AN AIRBNB HOST

In my area of Tokyo, Airbnb listings are not as common as hotels and traditional Japanese inns, ryokans (旅館), when it comes to accommodation choices for local travelers. Through conversations with my Japanese friends from various parts of the country, I've come to realize that when they visit Tokyo, they often prefer staying in hotels or ryokans, rather than booking through Airbnb. Interestingly, all the guests I've hosted so far have been from abroad, adding to the diverse and exciting experience of being an Airbnb host in Japan.

Being an Airbnb host has allowed me to share my love for Japan with travelers from around the world. It's incredibly fulfilling to witness the excitement of new groups of travelers and families as they make my Sangenjaya House their home for a few weeks while they explore the city. Their enthusiasm and curiosity about Japanese culture, the local neighborhood, and the vibrant city of Tokyo constantly reminds me of the beauty and charm that this country has to offer.

Each new guest brings their own unique stories and backgrounds, and I find it truly rewarding to provide them with a comfortable and welcoming space to experience Japan. As they immerse themselves in the local culture and traditions, I get to relive Japan through their eyes, sharing in their joy and discovery.

While hotels and ryokans may remain the preferred choice for many Japanese travelers, Airbnb has become a bridge connecting people from different parts of the world to experience the warmth and hospitality of Japan's homes. As an Airbnb host, I take great pride in introducing travelers to the local charms of my neighborhood and beyond, offering them a memorable and authentic stay that goes beyond the ordinary tourist experience.

It's a rewarding endeavor if you enjoy meeting and hosting people from around the world. As you navigate the path of obtaining a hotel license and venturing into the world of hospitality, remember that treating your neighbors, maintaining your house, and caring for your guests are all interconnected aspects that contribute to the overall success of your endeavor.

As I say often, be kind, be respectful, and have fun.

🔑 15

Renting Your Home Long-Term

While hosting an Airbnb can be lucrative it can also be time consuming, and if you're not excited about the idea of the hospitality business, hosting an Airbnb might not be the right fit for you. Another option is turning your newly renovated property into a long-term rental. Being a landlord of a long-term rental will give a lower financial return, but can be significantly less time consuming. The things you need to consider when renting a manshon apartment or a free-standing house long-term are very similar.

THINGS TO CONSIDER

Becoming a landlord in Japan can be a rewarding venture, both financially and culturally, but it comes with its own set of considerations. Here's a list of things to consider about being a landlord of a long-term rental.

Laws and Regulations

Acquaint yourself with Japan's real estate laws and regulations. Japan has specific laws governing landlord-tenant relationships, and it's essential to understand your responsibilities and obligations as a landlord. Engaging a local attorney or real estate broker can be a wise move to navigate these legal waters.

Property Management

Decide whether you'll manage the property yourself or hire a property management company. Managing it yourself may save you money, but it will require time and effort. Property management companies can handle everything from tenant screening to property maintenance, but they charge fees.

Tenant Screening

Finding reliable tenants is crucial. You'll want to conduct thorough background and credit checks on potential tenants. Ensuring they have a steady income and a clean rental history can help prevent future issues. Tenant screenings are more complex and time-consuming compared to many other countries, as selecting a tenant here is often likened to choosing a lifelong partner.

Furnishing and Maintenance

Consider whether you'll offer the apartment furnished or unfurnished. Either choice has its pros and cons. Maintenance is another key factor. Regular upkeep, repairs, and addressing tenant concerns promptly are vital for maintaining a positive landlord-tenant relationship.

Rental Agreements

Draft a comprehensive rental agreement. Japan has various types of rental contracts, but the standard fixed-term lease is common. Be clear about rent payment schedules, deposit terms, and responsibilities for repairs and utilities. Traditional rental contracts in Japan grant tenants significant power, making eviction a challenging process for landlords.

To address the challenges posed by standard contracts, many landlords are now turning to fixed-term lease agreements. These contracts have an expiration date but offer the possibility of renewal. However, with each renewal, conditions often change, typically resulting in rent increases. This trend provides landlords with more flexibility and predictability in the rental process.

Language Barrier

Communication can sometimes be a challenge, especially if you don't speak Japanese fluently. You might want to consider hiring a bilingual property manager or using translation services to facilitate communication.

Property Insurance

Ensure your property is adequately insured. Property insurance can protect your investment from damages caused by tenants or unforeseen events like natural disasters.

Tax Implications

Understand the tax implications of renting out your property. Japan has specific tax rules for rental income, so consult a tax professional to ensure compliance.

Cultural Considerations

Be aware of cultural differences that can impact your role as a landlord. For instance, Japanese tenants often expect a high level of privacy and respect from landlords.

Exit Strategy

Have an exit strategy in mind. If you decide to sell your property, consider factors like market conditions, capital gains tax, and the impact on your rental income.

Many of my friends, including Canadian Senpai and Isono-san, who both invest in older Japanese homes, take a straightforward and human approach to renting. They skip extensive tenant screenings and avoid charging renters unnecessary fees. Instead, they opt for a simple deposit system. As my friend Isono-san frequently emphasizes, having a landlord with DIY and renovation skills provides a sense of security for renters.

This approach leads to reduced tenant turnover, meaning less work for the landlord. Renters tend to stay for longer periods, in contrast to properties with exorbitant key money, gratitude money and other extraneous fees.

Returns on these older properties tend to improve as the building ages. In Tokyo, where a 10% return on investment (ROI) is considered excellent, my friend Isono-san's rental chart shows that he sometimes achieves returns of up to 40%. These exceptional returns are typically associated with older houses located a bit further away from the city's core.

Japan has strict tenant protection laws, ensuring that tenants' rights are respected. This adds an extra layer of security for both renters. (And is one of the reasons many landlords charge high fees and do excessive tenant screenings.) If you're looking for renters, platforms like Facebook Groups and Craigslist are options where you can create listings. However, my recommendation would be to work with a real estate broker for a smoother rental process.

Whether you choose a short-term or a long-term rental strategy for your renovated property, you'll want to make sure you maintain that investment over time. We'll explore that in the next chapter.

🔑 16

Maintaining Your Investment

Whether you've chosen to rent your renovated house long-term, or host it as an Airbnb, or simply decided to just live in it yourself, you'll want to make sure you maintain that investment. Home ownership comes with a set of responsibilities, and costs, including regular home maintenance, insurance, and of course—taxes.

HOME MAINTENANCE

This is the one place where being in Japan is not in your favor. The type of annual maintenance that is typical in the US and Europe isn't common in Japan. But I recommend you do maintain your property as you'll extend the life of the house you've renovated. While you can find many home maintenance lists online (and I suggest you find a more comprehensive list) there are two specific maintenance items you want to make sure to do regularly: check for water leaks, and check for termites.

Water Leaks

Water can be incredibly destructive to a building, and with the high humidity in Japan, once something gets wet it doesn't dry out, which can lead to mold and rot. Rot attracts termites and other wood-boring pests, so this is a double whammy if you don't stay on top of it. Check for signs of water leaks around sinks and toilets on a regular basis. You should also check for signs of water leaks around the window sills, roof, and any attic or crawl spaces. Finding, and fixing, any water leaks is crucial for maintaining your home long term.

Termites

Speaking of termites, that's the other thing you should do: check for signs of them. I'd check at least every six months, if not more frequently, as those formosan termites can quickly eat and damage the wood in your renovated home. While I've become familiar with termites, I'm no expert. However, there are a few telltale signs to watch for that might indicate an infestation:

- You see termite swarmers, either alive or dead in the building or nearby.
- You find mud shelter tubes on the outside or inside foundation walls, support piers, or plumbing under the house, or anywhere else on the interior or exterior of the house.
- You find a pile of small, uniform, brown pellets in a pile on the floor or a countertop. They look like a very large, coarse brown sand. This is a sign of an infestation as this pile is the dry fecal pellets from termites.

The reality is that once you see these signs, you already have an infestation and these pests have already done some damage to your home. Time to call a pro. You might also consider investing in termite treatment to prevent a termite infestation.

There's a lot more to home maintenance than what I've shared above, so I do encourage you to research more and create your own home maintenance list to maintain your property investments.

INSURANCE

Fire Insurance

One of the most comprehensive insurance policies you can get in Japan is ka-sai hoken (火災保険), fire insurance. Fire insurance in Japan is similar to most homeowner's insurance policies in the US, covers more than just damage from fires. When you rent or own a home in Japan, fire insurance is a must. In fact, many apartments require tenants to have fire insurance as part of their leasing contracts.

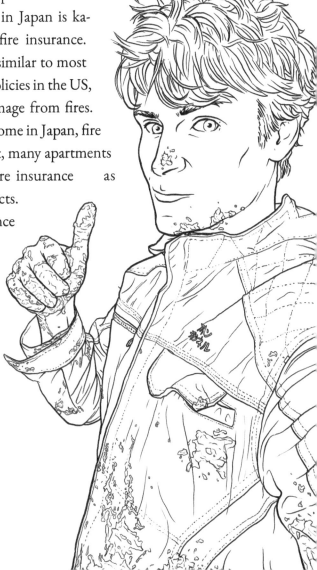

In essence, fire insurance covers your cherished belongings in the event of damage caused by fire, smoke, and more. Importantly, it also typically covers other damages resulting from common occurrences such as:

- Accidents like a child breaking your computer or damaging antique pottery you've collected.
- Appliance mishaps, like your washing machine overflowing and affecting both your floor and your neighbor's unit below.
- Unforeseen incidents, such as accidentally injuring someone while pursuing your hobbies, like playing soccer.

On average, fire insurance in Japan costs between ¥20,000–¥40,000 ($138–$276) for a two-year policy. The price may vary depending on any additional coverage options you choose. Consult an insurance provider for precise pricing and potential add-ons to tailor your policy to your needs. Your broker can help you with an introduction.

Fire insurance coverage typically encompasses three main categories:

Home Contents

Designed to safeguard your possessions, with the cost of your policy determined based on the value of your belongings. This is typically structured in broad groupings rather than as an itemized plan, which is more common in other countries.

Tenant Liability

This coverage extends to accidents causing damage inside the home or even to your neighbor's units. It can include scenarios like overflowing bathtubs or kitchen mishaps.

Personal Liability

An essential part of your insurance plan, personal liability covers situations where someone's property is damaged or they are injured due to an accident involving you or negligence on your part. For instance, if you're in a bike accident and collide with someone on the street, this part of your insurance would cover medical costs and property damages for the other party.

Some employers offer insurance to their international employees on temporary contracts in Japan. Ensure you verify your coverage details with your employer. Even with employer-provided coverage, you might still want to consider adding a Japanese fire insurance policy to ensure comprehensive coverage for household emergencies and accidents.

While fire insurance is essential, it's essential to understand that

🔑

I strongly advise considering at least the essential fire insurance, and don't let the name mislead you. While it's called "fire insurance," it offers comprehensive coverage for various unforeseen events, ensuring your peace of mind.

If you're obtaining a loan through a Japanese bank they will often require you to have fire insurance in place. Even if you purchase a more affordable property outright, I would highly recommend securing insurance for your home. It's a vital step in safeguarding your investment and ensuring that you're prepared for any unexpected challenges that may arise.

it doesn't typically cover natural disasters, such as earthquakes. For this purpose, there is a separate option aptly named earthquake insurance.

Earthquake Insurance

Living in Japan necessitates preparedness for earthquakes. However, standard fire insurance policies do not cover earthquake-related damage, including fire damage resulting from earthquakes. Therefore, it's crucial to supplement your policy with earthquake insurance, which is available as an add-on.

The cost of earthquake insurance varies by prefecture. Fees start at around ¥6,500 ($45) and can go up to approximately ¥41,100 ($283) per year per ¥10 million (~$69,000) of insured property according to Japan's Ministry of Finance. You can refer to their website for specific details on pricing in your area *(the URL is in the "More Information" chapter at the end of the book)*.

Earthquake insurance is exclusively for earthquake-related disasters. It covers the loss of personal items, including household goods, as well as property damage caused by earthquakes, volcanic eruptions, and tsunamis, including fire, destruction, landslides, and water damage resulting from these events.

Please keep in mind that earthquake coverage typically excludes items such as precious metals, jewels, and antiques valued at more than ¥300,000 ($2,070) per item or per set.

TAXES

Owning real estate in Japan comes with the responsibility of paying two annual taxes: the Fixed Asset Tax and the City Planning Tax. These property taxes apply whether you're an individual or a corporation.

Fixed Asset Tax

This tax is calculated based on the assessed value of your fixed assets, which include land, houses, and depreciable assets. The tax rate (as of 2023) is 1.4% of the assessed value of your fixed assets, and is paid to the local city, town or village, or the Tokyo Metropolitan Government for properties within Tokyo's twenty-three wards.

City Planning Tax

The City Planning Tax is levied to fund city planning and land readjustment projects.

The taxable properties are the land and buildings within designated urbanization promotion areas as per the City Planning Act. The tax rate (as of 2023) is 0.3% of the assessed value of fixed assets (with variations across municipalities). Again, these taxes are paid to the local city, town or village, or the Tokyo Metropolitan Government for properties within Tokyo's twenty-three wards.

The owner is responsible for paying these taxes—whoever the owner is as of January 1st each year is the taxpayer for that year. If the property changes ownership during the year, the tax amount is usually divided proportionally between the seller and buyer.

These property taxes are due four times a year, with different deadlines set by each municipality. Late payments incur additional charges. Payment methods vary but are typically outlined in the tax notice, which can be settled at banks, post offices, financial institutions, or even designated convenience stores.

Income Tax

Both residents and non-residents are subject to income tax in Japan. The financial year ends on December 31st, with tax statements and payments due by March 15th of the following year. Some things to keep in mind:

- Most western countries have tax treaties with Japan to prevent double taxation, so check if your country has such an agreement before investing in Japanese properties.
- Once you meet the minimum reporting threshold, you must file tax returns and can claim deductions, but this requires filing the property purchase within the first year.
- Income tax rates in Japan are progressive, meaning the percentage increases with higher income.

Purchase Tax

This one-time payment is around 2.5% of the property purchase price and is based on the official property valuation. Payment occurs within 6–24 months after purchasing the home.

Capital Gains Tax

Rates vary depending on the duration of property ownership, with different rates for residents and non-residents.

For residents of Japan:

- **If held less than 5 years:** 30% income tax + 9% municipal tax + 2.1% Tohoku reconstruction tax [*]
- **If held for more than 5 years:** 15% income tax + 5% municipal tax + 2.1% Tohoku reconstruction tax

---

[*] If you're curious about the Tohoku reconstruction tax, there's an interesting article linked in the "More Information" chapter.

For non-residents:

- **If held less than five years:** 30% income tax + 2.1% Tohoku reconstruction tax
- **If held for more than five years:** 15% income tax + 2.1% Tohoku reconstruction tax

Consumption Tax

This tax is currently 10% and is included in most quotes and invoices for goods and services in Japan.

Gift/Inheritance Tax

Inheritance tax in Japan is calculated per person and is levied on all assets bequeathed to beneficiaries. For foreign residents, only Japanese assets are taxable. The tax rates range from 15% to 55% depending on the taxable amount.

Navigating these taxes requires careful planning and adherence to local regulations. Consulting with tax professionals or legal experts can provide valuable guidance, ensuring compliance and potentially optimizing your financial situation. Remember that tax laws can change, so staying updated and seeking professional advice is advisable to make informed decisions regarding your real estate investments in Japan.

MANAGEMENT FEES

When you own apartments or condominiums in Japan, you may also be required to pay building management fees. These fees cover the maintenance and operation of the shared spaces and facilities within the building, such as elevators, common areas, and security services. Building management fees are typically charged on a monthly or annual basis and are separate from the property taxes mentioned earlier. It's essential to budget for these fees as part of your overall property ownership expenses.

DON'T LET YOUR INVESTMENT BECOME AN AKIYA

Paying taxes is a given, and insuring your home in the event of fire, earthquakes and other natural disasters is simply a smart way to protect your investment. Maintaining your renovated property through regular home maintenance extends the life of your investment. If you're planning on potentially selling your property in the future you want to keep it looking new, and even if you plan on maintaining ownership, those you rent to will appreciate that you keep your houses looking new, and well-maintained.

🔑 17

Looking Forward

I f you've read this book until now, you're on your way to understanding the Japanese real estate landscape, particularly when it
comes to older properties and akiyas. By this point, you grasp the
hurdles and potential benefits. If you're willing to invest time, en-
gage with the community, and keep learning, this path could be
right for you. If you haven't noticed yet, I'll point out that the words
"passive income" haven't been mentioned one single time in this
book. (Well, until now.) Renovating houses is a rewarding, but not
"passive" endeavor. You could hire people to do all the jobs for you,
but DIY and renovating on my own, combined with hiring the right
professionals, gives me a lot of joy and saves a lot of money.

Through dedication, persistence, and an incredible community,
I've turned abandoned properties into beautiful homes. Sangenjaya
House, in particular, has become an internet sensation, showing the
process and the beauty of preserving Japan's unique architecture
with the world. This journey has taught me the value of preserv-

ing history and the joy of turning neglected spaces into cherished homes. I look forward to continuing this passion for akiyas and contributing to the preservation of Japan's cultural heritage.

Documenting the renovation process on my Japanese-language YouTube channel opened up a whole new world of possibilities. Hundreds of Japanese people reached out to me, seeking guidance and inspiration for their own akiyas. They were intrigued by the idea that renovation and maintenance were not only possible but also a financially viable option for older properties.

Continuing the journey on my English-language channel, *Anton in Japan*, has opened the door on this amazing world to an even wider audience. Through my videos, I aim to showcase the potential and charm of these abandoned houses and demonstrate that they could be transformed into beautiful, functional homes. I encourage others to embrace the concept of renovating and preserving traditional Japanese houses, even if they require some tender loving care.

This positive response from my viewers has only fueled my passion for this niche in the real estate market. I realized that by sharing my experiences and insights, I could empower others to explore the untapped potential of abandoned properties in Japan.

Japan is battling their declining population and the number of empty houses is rising. The opportunities, especially if you are ready and willing to get your hands dirty, for renovating old houses are massive. I suggest you ask yourself, in the end, what do you want out of your life? Do you want to move to Japan? Do you want to invest your money into Japan? Do you want to spend your precious time in Japan? Do you want to find and renovate old "free" houses in Japan? If you do, make sure you stay respectful, curious, and immerse yourself into the local community, and this wonderful country.

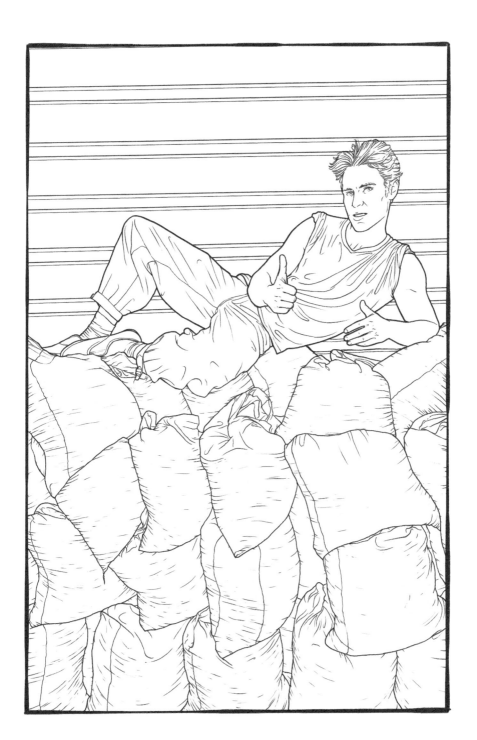

Japan offers incredible attractions like mountains, hot springs, temples, skiing and even surfing. The food is fantastic, the culture is amazing, and so many things are extremely convenient here—except for getting rid of renovation trash. Tokyo, being the largest city in the world, has so many things to explore and so many different and interesting areas across the city, all available within a few subway stops. It's a very clean, and very safe city to visit, enjoy, and live.

Or maybe you prefer the idea of living in a rural area of Japan, where you can find an akiya that can offer even more for your money. Entering the Japanese akiya real estate market can unlock many opportunities. Both my Tree House and Sangenjaya House are examples, along with all the examples and stories from friends. The opportunities are real, and if you're familiar with DIY renovations and can dedicate time, Japan holds a world of opportunity for you. Come visit and experience the culture. Learn the Japanese language. Be curious, be respectful, and maybe you too will be able to purchase a "free house in Japan."

Part 5
RESOURCES

NOTE TO THE READER

Japanese has three different character sets, kanji, katakana and hiragana. All are correct, and usage depends primarily on the source of the word. Kanji are ideographic characters from Chinese that have been adapted into Japanese. The word "kanji" literally means "chinese character." There are over 50,000 kanji characters and each one has a specific meaning. Hiragana and katakana are phonetic alphabets, developed in the 5th and 9th centuries, respectively. Each character in hiragana and katakana represents a phonetic sound. Hiragana is traditionally used for Japanese words, and katakana is traditionally used for non-Japanese words. In general, if there is kanji available for a word, and the writer knows the kanji, then kanji is used, but all character sets are correct and all are used widely in Japan.

🔑 18

Glossary

SWEDISH

hemnetknarka - literally "high on the drug of Hemnet," referring to Sweden's biggest property site, Hemnet, and "knark," meaning "to be on drugs" akiya (空き家 or アキヤ) - abandoned or vacant house

JAPANESE

akiya (空き家 or アキヤ) - abandoned or vacant house

akiya bank (空き家バンク) - a database of listings for abandoned or vacant houses

akiya toushi (空き家投資) - the art of investing in abandoned homes

apaato (アパート) - a small, inexpensively built apartment building, usually two-story with multiple apartments that are for rent only and tend to be very small, cheap and not sound-proofed in any way

Atami (熱海市) - a small city, about 36,000 residents, situated on the side of a partially submerged volcanic caldera on the edge of Sagami Bay, known for its warm climate, fireworks, and onsen hot springs

Chiba (千葉県) - a prefecture east of Tokyo on Japan's eastern coast with a population of about 6.2 million, part of the greater Tokyo area

Chiba (千葉市) - the capital city of Chiba Prefecture, about 40 km (25 mi) east of Tokyo on Tokyo Bay

choko choko (ちょこちょこ) - little by little, piece by piece

chukai tesuryou (仲介手数料) - one-time agent fee paid to the real estate agent for helping you find a rental property

chuukou ikkodate (中古 一戸建て) - a used house, meaning a previously owned house

engawa (縁側) - a veranda-like space often found in traditional homes, providing a seamless transition between indoor and outdoor areas

fusuma (ふすま) - a framed and papered sliding door used to partition off rooms

Futako-Tamagawa (二子玉川) - the area surrounding Futa-ko-Tamagawa Station, often referring to the Tamagawa and Seta districts of Setagaya on the southern border of Tokyo

gaijin (外人) - literally means "outside person"; foreigners and non-Japanese citizens

gaijin (外人) **card** - colloquialism meaning that foreigners don't know how to do things correctly, from the Alien Registration Card that foreigners staying longer than 90 days were required to carry prior to 2012

gaikokujin (外国人) - the politically correct way to refer to a foreigner, with the additional character for "country" inserted between "outside" and "person"

genkan (玄関) - traditional entryway of Japanese homes, typically a step lower than the floor level of the rest of the house

gomen (ごめん) - sorry

gomi yashiki (ゴミ屋敷) - "garbage house," a building (usually a residence) or land being incorrectly used as a refuse dump

hanko (はんこ) - a carved stamp used by an individual (or individual representing a company) to guarantee a signature or initials, used interchangeably with inkan

Harajuku (原宿) - a district in Shibuya known as a center of Japanese youth culture and fashion

hikkoshi hiyou (引越し費用) - fee for a moving company

hinoki (檜) - cypress wood

hinoyoujin (火の用心) - "be careful about fire"

hoken (保険) - insurance

Hokkaido (北海道) - Japan's second largest island, the capital city of Hokkaido is Sapporo (Tokyo is the capital city of Japan)

Homukyoku (法務局) - Japan Legal Affairs Bureau

hoshou gaisha tesuryou (保証会社手数料) - guarantor fee for when a renter uses a hired company to be the guarantor on their rental contract

ikkodate (戸建て) - free-standing house

inkan (いんかん) - a carved stamp used by an individual (or individual representing a company) to guarantee a signature or initials, used interchangeably with hanko

isshaku (一尺) - unit of measurement, one shaku, ~30.3 cm (~1 ft)

issun (一寸) - unit of measurement, one sun, ~3.03 cm (~1.2 in)

izakaya (居酒屋) - a type of informal bar that serves alcoholic drinks and snacks, similar to a pub or tavern

jiko bukken (事故物件) - a property where someone has been injured or died in a sudden, violent or tragic way such as suicide, murder, fire, or neglect

jou koukan hi (錠交換費) - lock exchange fee, ensures you have new locks and keys for your rental

Kanagawa (神奈川県) - the second-most populous prefecture of Japan with 9.2 million people, bordering Tokyo to the north and a popular tourist area, the political and economic center of Japan from 1185 to 1333

Kamogawa (鴨川市) - a city in Chiba at the mount of the Kamogawa river with approximately 32,000 people, home to Mount Kiyosumi, the highest point in Chiba

karaoke (カラオケ) - literally means "empty orchestra," a type of entertainment offered in clubs and bars where people sing along to recorded music

keitora (軽トラ) - kei truck, a mini pickup truck, also known as a "light truck"

kasai (火災) - fire

kasai hoken (火災保険 or かさいほけん) - fire insurance

kawara (かわら) - clay roof tiles

kenpeiritsu (建坪率) - a regulation governing how much land can be covered by a building

kimono (きもの) - a long, loose robe with wide sleeves and tied with a sash, originally worn as a formal garment

kinjo kaichō (近所会長) - a neighborhood association president

kinshi (禁止) - banned, forbidden

kiri (桐) - Paulownia wood, specifically P. tomentosa, the "princess tree"

kiri tansu（桐タンス）- paulownia wood kimono chests.

kominka（古民家）- literally "old house", a traditional folk house, usually defined as buildings "built before 1950 using traditional architectural methods"

kotatsu（こたつ）- a low, heated table covered with a thick blanket

koushinryou（更新料）- lease renewal fee

kyoka（許可）- permission

kyoubai（競売）- auction

kyoubai bukken（競売物件）- real estate property that has been repossessed by the court to be sold at auction when the property owner defaults on a loan in which the property was used for collateral

kyouekihi（共益費）- a maintenance fee

manshon（マンション）- a multi-family residential building at least three-stories high and typically constructed using steel-reinforced concrete, similar to an urban condominium building in the US or Europe

minpaku（民泊 or みんぱく）- a private short-stay accommodation or lodging, such as an Airbnb

minpaku kinshi（民泊 禁止）- short term rentals forbidden

moshikomi（申し込み）- the written application to purchase a home, similar to a written offer in the United States

mottainai (もったいない) - "what a waste," an expression of regret over a wasteful use, situation or result

miyadaiku (宮大工) - traditional Japanese carpentry using elaborate wooden joints rather than mechanical fasteners, also the carpenters who practice this type of carpentry

Muji (無印良品) - retailer which sells a wide variety of household and consumer goods, with an emphasis on minimalism, recycling, reducing waste and a no-logo or "no-brand" policy

muri (むり) - impossible, used as an expression of frustration, "this is impossible!"

Nagano (長野市) - the capital and largest city of Nagano Prefecture, categorized as a core city, surrounded by mountains and famous for the mountain-based onsens, or hot springs

Nakameguro (中目黒) - a residential district of Meguro, Tokyo, famous for it's cherry-blossom viewing and it's unique boutique cafes and shops

nishaku (二尺) - unit of measurement, ~60.6 cm (~2 ft)

nissun (二寸) - unit of measurement, ~6.06 cm (~2.4 in)

nori (海苔 or のり) - dried edible seaweed used as a wrapper around sushi rolls or onigiri

Obon (お盆) - annual Buddhist event in August for commemorating one's ancestors, whose spirits are believed to temporarily return to this world in order to visit their relatives

oden (御田) - fish cake stew, a one-pot dish with several ingredients such as boiled eggs, daikon, konjac, processed fish cakes and dashi

ofuro (お風呂) - bath

okonomiyaki (お好み焼き) - a savory pancake dish consisting of wheat flour batter and other ingredients cooked on a teppan, flat iron griddle

omiyage (お土産) - gift

onachenji (オーナーチェンジ) - owner change

onigiri (御握り or おにぎり) - white rice formed into triangular or cylindrical shapes, often with a filling and wrapped in nori

onsen (温泉) - hot springs and the traditional ins and bathing facilities around them of which there are ~3,000 establishments and ~25,000 hot spring sources throughout Japan

oshibori (おしぼり) - a hot wet hand towel for cleaning your hands before eating

oshiire (押し入れ) - closet or storage area

reikin (礼金) - gift money, or key money, literally means "gratitude money"

reikon (霊魂) - the human soul

rifo mu manshon (リフォ無 マンション) - a renovated manshon apartment

rotenburo (露天風呂) - an outdoor bath

ryokan (旅館) - a traditional Japanese inn

sai kenchi fukanou (再建築不可能) - a non-rebuildable property, typically located on narrow streets

Secchan (せっちゃん) - one of Anton's favorite restaurants in Japan (For my special secret list of places to visit in Tokyo, come to anton.jp/booktalk)

senpai (先輩) - a senpai is a person who is in a higher position than you in terms of skill, age, experience or social status, someone who can guide you, a mentor

sento (銭湯) - a communal bathhouse where customers pay for entrance

Setagaya (世田谷区) - a special ward in Tokyo along with the named neighborhood within that ward, the largest population ward in Tokyo with ~950,000 people

shakkanhō (尺貫法) - traditional Japanese measurement system

shaku (尺) - a unit of measurement, also known as the "Japanese foot," ~30.3 cm (~ 1 ft)

Shibuya Crossing (渋谷スクランブル交差点) - a popular pedestrian "scramble" crossing in Shibuya in front of Shibuya Station where vehicles are stopped in all directions to allow pedestrians to use the entire intersection

Shinjuku (新宿区) - a special ward in Tokyo, a major commercial and administrative center

shin-taishin (新耐震) - New Earthquake Resistant Building Standard Amendment, created after the 1978 Miyagi earthquake that damaged or destroyed over 6,000 homes

Shimokitazawa (下北沢) - a neighborhood in Setagaya, located in the southwestern corner of the district

shihō shoshi (司法書士) - legal scrivener, similar to a notary public in the United States

shikikin (敷金) - security deposit for renting an apartment

shinchiku ikkodate (新築 一戸建て) - newly built free-standing house

shinkansen (新幹線) - Japan's high-speed train

shoki seisou hi (初期清掃費) - cleaning fee

Shōwa era (昭和時代) - period corresponding to the reign of Emperor Shōwa (Hirohito) from December 25, 1926, until his death on January 7, 1989

sodai gomi (粗大ごみ) - oversized garbage

sun (寸) - unit of measurement, ~3.03 cm (~ 1.193 in), there are 10 sun in 1 shaku

Takken (宅建) - exam, a qualification that must be obtained to buy or sell real estate as a licensed broker

tatami (たたみ) - a type of mat used as a floor covering in traditional Japanese rooms, also used as a unit of measurement, ~1.91 x 0.95 m (~6 ft 3 in x 3 ft 1 in)

tawaamanshon (タワーマンション) - a tower mansion, a very tall building of condominiums

teppan (鉄板) - a flat iron grill, or griddle

teppanyaki (鉄板焼き) - a style of cooking that uses a flat iron grill, or griddle, to cook ingredients in the center of the dining table

tokonoma (床の間) - a recessed space in a reception room used to display art or artistic items, a space of honor and aesthetic appreciation

tsubo (坪) - unit of measurement commonly used for land and houses, ~3.3 m2 (~35.5 ft2)

tsuchikabe (つちかべ) - traditional wall construction method using earth and straw to create thick walls, providing excellent insulation and ventilation

warukatta ne (悪かったね) - "that was bad of me"

yōkai (妖怪) - strange apparition, monster

Yokohama (横浜) - second-largest city in Japan, capital city of Kanagawa Prefecture, with ~3.8 million people, on Tokyo Bay, a major economic, cultural, high-tech, and commercial hub of the greater Tokyo area

yoroshiku onegai shimasu (よろしくお願いします) - a customary saying when you meet someone, meaning "I'm looking forward to having good relations with you"

yosekiritsu (容積率) - a building regulation that defines the maximum usable floorspace in the buildings on the piece of property

yurei (幽霊) - ghost, literally "faint soul"

Yūtenji (祐天寺) - temple of the Pure Land Buddhism in Nakameguro built in 1718, also the name of a residential district adjacent to the temple

🔑 19

More Information

ANTON

- Website: https://www.anton.jp/
- Email: info@anton.jp
- Instagram: https://www.instagram.com/antonwormann/

YOUTUBE

- English-language channel: https://youtube.com/@antoninjapan
- Japanese-language channel: https://youtube.com/@antonwormann/
- Playlist for Tokyo Renovation Diaries https://www.youtube.com/playlist?list=PL_4tRHMzlAqBDJRzjTxdUv3sYWhtRBdF2

HOME TOURS

- Tree House tour from Caleb Simpson: https://youtu.be/yQBScME822Y
- Sangenjaya House tour from Caleb Simposon: https://youtu.be/2C6XxjgXLcl
- Things left at Sangenjaya House: https://www.youtube.com/watch?v=GGv-PkNblGc
- The termites: https://youtu.be/ap2ocwqtBnk
- Trash & the kei truck: https://www.youtube.com/watch?v=NZ60J0n5a4Q
- Example of walls around an akiya: https://youtu.be/V0rbcVCUBOk
- Ito-san's akiya: https://youtu.be/XNnV6EDoCqc
- Ito-san interview: https://youtu.be/MU7Y81-BvTQ

LANGUAGE & CULTURE STUDY

- Italki.com - https://www.italki.com
- DuoLingo - https://www.duolingo.com
- Rosetta Stone - https://www.rosettastone.com
- More information on Japanese cultural beliefs around ghosts: http://www.deepjapan.org/a/4147 (also many articles about experiencing Japan as a local)
- More information about Japanese writing & characters: https://www.japaneseexplorer.com.sg/japanese-writing/ and https://8020japanese.com/japanese-characters-explained/

CONNECTIONS & COMMUNITY

- Building and Renovating a House in Japan - https://www.facebook.com/groups/899232140163288
- Tokyo Expat Network - https://www.facebook.com/groups/TokyoExpatNetwork
- "Sayonara Sales" groups
- https://www.facebook.com/groups/TokyoSSTO
- https://www.facebook.com/groups/TRF.sayonara
- https://www.facebook.com/groups/276330006172808
- Quintet Vinyl Bar: 〒154-0022 Tokyo, Setagaya City, Umegaoka, 1 Chome-15-9, SPACE88 (スペース88)
- (For my special secret list of places to visit in Tokyo, come to anton.jp/booktalk)

SHORT-TERM ACCOMMODATIONS

- Sangenjaya House: https://www.houseintokyo.com/ or https://www.airbnb.com/rooms/872705568173319685
- Atami Villa (Ken): https://www.airbnb.co.uk/rooms/633145280679993392
- Muji Base: https://www.airbnb.com/rooms/904742087208633715

LONG-TERM ACCOMMODATIONS & HOUSING ASSISTANCE

- Erik Nas Nasriddinov, E-Housing: https://www.e-housing.jp/
- Suumo: https://suumo.jp/

- AtHome: https://www.athome.co.jp/
- REINS: https://system.reins.jp/
- Hemnet: https://www.hemnet.se/
- Zillow: https://www.zillow.com/
- Real Estate Exam Information: https://japanbox.jp/useful_life/3312/?lang=en

BANKS OPEN TO FOREIGNERS

- SMBC - https://www.smbc.co.jp/global/
- Star Ginko - https://www.tokyostarbank.co.jp/profile/en/
- SONY Bank - https://sonybank.net/en/corp/
- Rakuten - https://www.rakuten-bank.co.jp/english/account/opening/

AKIYA BANKS

- Home's: https://www.homes.co.jp/akiyabank/
- At Home: https://www.akiya-athome.jp/
- List of Akiya Databases: https://resources.realestate.co.jp/buy/akiya-banks-in-japan-links-to-vacant-house-databases-by-prefecture/

ESTATE CLEANING & LIQUIDATION

- Forever: https://www.for-ever.jp

HOUSEWARES, HOME CENTERS & BUILDING MATERIALS

- IKEA: https://www.ikea.com/
- Muji: https://www.muji.com/
- Yahoo! Auctions: https://auctions.yahoo.co.jp/
- Tokyo Craigslist: https://tokyo.craigslist.org/?lang=en
- KOHNAN PRO - https://www.hc-kohnan.com
- Super Viva Home - https://www.vivahome.co.jp
- CAINZ HOME - https://www.cainz.com
- Cedar Tubs: https://www.cedartubs.com/
- Rustoleum Tub & TIle Refinishing Kit: https://www.rustoleum.com/product-catalog/consumer-brands/specialty/tub-and-tile-refinishing-kit

JAPANESE GOVERNMENT AGENCIES

- Ministry of Justice: https://www.moj.go.jp/ENGLISH/top_index.html
- Legal Affairs Bureau: https://www.moj.go.jp/ENGLISH/m_hisho06_00034.html
- Ministry of Land, Infrastructure, Transport, and Tourism: https://www.mlit.go.jp/en/
- Ministry of Finance. https://www.mof.go.jp/english/index.htm
- More information about the Tohoku reconstruction tax: https://www.japantimes.co.jp/news/2023/03/09/national/politics-diplomacy/reconstruction-tax-stir-debate/

INSPIRATION

- Kengo Kuma: https://kkaa.co.jp/en/
- Tadao Ando: http://www.tadao-ando.com/

INSTAGRAM INSPIRATION

- @dylaniwakuni - https://www.instagram.com/dylaniwakuni/
- @Chantarokichi - https://www.instagram.com/chantarokichi/
- @japanesethatchingguy - https://www.instagram.com/japanesethatchingguy/
- @Japanpropertycentral - https://www.instagram.com/japanpropertycentral/
- @Tokyobuild - https://www.instagram.com/tokyobuild/
- @Jeremytsa - https://www.instagram.com/jeremytsa/
- @Cheaphousesjapan - https://www.instagram.com/cheaphousesjapan/

You can get a 20% discount on their newsletter services using my code at www.cheaphousesjapan.com/Anton

How This Story Continues

I absolutely love life in Japan. Best powder snow in the world, fantastic beaches, surfing, and it is safe. Renovation work, making videos, and connecting Japan with the world brings me so much joy. Being surrounded by wonderful people, staying healthy, enjoying delicious food, and working out daily keeps me inspired. I'm always up for new challenges and learning something new—whether it's mastering a skill, writing, improving my Japanese, or exploring historic houses. Tokyo's vibrant energy feels like home to me, and I'm here to stay.

People ask me, "Why don't you keep your experiences to yourself and keep this valuable information and insights to a select few?" My answer is simple: I enjoy teaching. There are 8.5 million abandoned houses in Japan. Eight and a half million. And this number keeps growing. While I am not in a position to discuss immigration in Japan, I believe it's inevitable that Japan will ease its immigration laws soon due to its aging population and the need to bring more people into the country to take care of all of these empty homes.

I'm passionate about sharing my knowledge in Japanese real estate and renovation, particularly when it comes to old, inexpensive, and neglected houses that most traditional real estate brokers and developers in Japan avoid. And things are already changing. Recently one of the most luxurious real estate agencies in Tokyo—an agency with over twenty years of experience—came to me for advice about akiya investing because they don't know anything about this market and want to learn more.

As you can tell, I'm very passionate about sharing my experiences in Japan and my house renovations. Sustainability is gaining momentum in Japan, and as awareness continues to grow, I believe the trend of renovating older homes will become increasingly popular. I aspire to be a part of this movement. I can't tackle Japan's vacant house problem alone, but by inspiring and educating people interested in the world of akiyas and Japan, where information is already limited even to Japanese citizens, I genuinely hope more people will recognize the charm of renovating and reviving old Japanese houses.

My next step in this journey is to create exciting educational media content focused on investing in akiyas. This content aims to inspire both foreigners and Japanese individuals to transform rundown houses into something beautiful. To be the first to hear about it, please sign up for my newsletter at www.anton.jp.

There's a special feeling about Japan that's hard to put into words. It's like being a kid who doesn't want to leave a fun party and asks to stay a bit longer. That's how I feel about Japan—I just want to stay here and keep enjoying every moment.

I'll keep creating content, being creative, sharing knowledge, taking care of myself, and embracing new learning experiences.

Thank you for reading my book about my journey renovating

houses here in Japan. Thank you for your millions of views on my channels, your tens of thousands of comments, your curiosity, and all your lovely messages. You made the writing of the first ever En-glish-language book about akiya and the opportunities within cheap Japanese real estate incredibly fun.

I truly appreciate you. There's more to come.

これからも皆様のお世話になる事と思います
ご指導、ご教示の程何卒よろしくお願い申し上げます

Kore kara mo mina sama no osewa ni naru koto to omoimasu go shido, go kyouji no hodo nani tozo yoroshiku onegai moushiage-masu.

(With gratitude,)
Anton Wörmann

Anton in Japan
www.anton.jp